cheeky treats

Cheeky treats

BRILLIANT BAKES AND CAKES

LIAM CHARLES

HODDER &
STOUGHTON

CONTENTS

INTRODUCTION

'Ello 'ello 'ello, Liam here. How's it going? Seriously, I want you to reply – this book has been designed to be a conversation! Throughout the book I'll be guiding you through the recipes, telling you stories and, of course, cracking jokes. But, before all of that, let me take you back to 2013 …

I'll admit I've always had an incredibly sweet tooth. Anything remotely sweet, sign me up – chocolate cake, sweet potatoes or even chewing gum (it has to be bubble mint flavour, though). And, for as long as I can remember, food programmes have been my life. Mum would get so annoyed with me – the TV planner was infested with them. Indulging in so many food programmes eventually led me to put my obsession into practice and I made my first ever cupcakes with a family friend – they were dense, flat and green. They had a good flavour, though. It was lemon – zingy, innit?

Even though they weren't the best cupcakes in the world (cough, cough), it took just that one bake to show me that I could express myself creatively, whether through flavour combinations or concepts. And I was hooked.

One thing I'll say, as soon as I'm interested in something, I want to know every nook and cranny of it. So I began to teach myself the basics of baking. Yes, there were tonnes of mistakes but getting it wrong is all part of the process – then when you get it right, the feeling is insane. There are no rules – you have to learn a lot of techniques and discover different ingredients but the best part is when you develop your own style. Coming from Caribbean descent, I try to turn traditional Caribbean meals into modern bakes. Not too difficult … Gulp.

Saying all that, I've definitely been influenced by a lot of people – they are people close to my heart who are widely recognised in their craft. Big love to Heston Blumenthal, Dominque Ansel and Christina Tosi – and I could go on and on and on … All those chefs have a

distinctive style, use amazing flavour combinations and have super cool concepts. Closer to home, though, my nan, Cynthia, is the cook of all cooks. I mean it. Her flavours are just … ahh!

Two other people who have had a huge impact on me, even if they haven't exactly influenced my work physically, are Benoit Blin and Cherish Finden. With them it stems deeper than influence – spending time with them earlier this year has helped me appreciate cooking and baking so much more than I did before. The way they talk about food is truly inspirational. Look at me getting all emotional!

HOW I WRITE MY RECIPES

Let us delve into the mind of Liam to see how I come up with my recipe ideas … Firstly, I draw inspiration from my surroundings – you'll care most about what you're baking if you do that. Next, depending on the inspiration, I decide whether it's going to be sweet or savoury, a pie, a cake, a tart, etc. Then I ask myself what I'm currently eating and enjoying, or what is interesting me. Finally, to enhance the flavour, I'll think about and look for complimentary ingredients. So, now we have the form, the flavours and finally the finesse – the overall concept of the bake. Attach a meaning to anything in life and it will take your work to another level. FACT.

I always draw my bakes first with annotations. This is just to ensure it's clear in my head visually. I often draw each component separately, too, a bit like an exploded jigsaw puzzle – to see what fits, what doesn't, or what's missing.

I'd been inventing, sketching and baking for three years before applying for *Bake Off*. I thought that it was the best thing an amateur baker could achieve. I must admit, I can be my own worst enemy and there are times when I overthink things and doubt myself, but going on *Bake Off* helped me tackle that. It showed me that once you put your mind to something, no matter how long it takes, you'll get there (I know, I know, you've probably heard it a million times). Most importantly, though, I felt there had been a certain stigma related to baking, that it was only for mums and young kids. Well, not anymore.

When I bake it always seems to be for a crowd, but it's perfectly possible to halve the quantities in lots of the recipes and, for example, make a two-layer cake not a four-layer one or have half the number of biscuits. Not sure why you'd want to of course but that's just me …

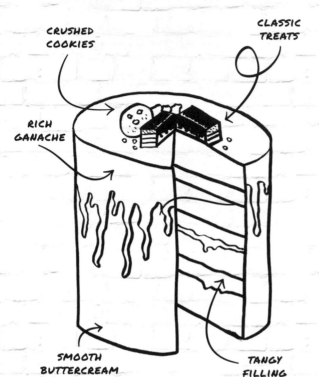

CRUSHED COOKIES

CLASSIC TREATS

RICH GANACHE

SMOOTH BUTTERCREAM

TANGY FILLING

HOW DOES THE BOOK WORK?

The book is broken down into five sections: Sweet, Savoury, Nostalgia, Simple and just outright Celebrate. The recipes are a mixture of all the different things that got me ticking from the get go. RECIPES FOR ALL, WOOP!

The number one rule of the book is that you have to follow each recipe exactly or else this book will self-destruct in 3 … 2 … 1 …

Nah, I'm being silly. When it comes to the actual foundations of the bakes (for example, the sponge, biscuits or pastry itself), definitely follow the proportions as listed but, in terms of the flavour of the fillings and the design of the bake, feel free to express yourself! There are times when I've suggested how to decorate something or I've told you what flavour to make your filling but, you know, swap the orange for that lime, add a textured surface to the cake or even come up with a new filling for the pies. Let me know how you get on.

THE CHEEKIEST OF TOP TIPS

I. Always read the recipe
Always read the recipe a couple of times before you start, bud. You might need to prepare a few components beforehand. Sounds silly but there are times, even now, I'll skim a recipe once, then halfway through making it … Oh, sugar! No pun intended.

2. Get out your kit and ingredients
Make sure you have everything out that you need, ready to use. The last thing you want is to have to go through drawers and all sorts in the middle of a bake. You don't have to do this (I'm a little bit weird) but I buy my ingredients a couple of days before I'm going to bake. You wanna be super organised when you bake, it'll show through in your final result.

3. Get friends, family and neighbours involved
Whether it's tasting or helping you out in the kitchen, you will become a better baker with their help.

4. Write × draw × share ideas
At least once a month, spend the whole day going to supermarkets, markets, pop-ups and bakeries. Get inspired.

5. Ultimate tip
Wash up as you go along × have fun!

WHAT YOU NEED TO START

When I first started baking, I had a couple of different-sized bowls, old-school scales, cake tins, spoons and a free-standing mixer (because luckily my mum used to bake back in the day). As I began to get better, I bought myself more decorating kit – a cake turntable, a cake leveller, baking and tart tins in various sizes, electric scales, loads of piping nozzles, food thermometers and a food-processor – you name it!

Now, promise me one thing: don't get lost in the caramel sauce. What I mean by that is, baking can be extremely exciting but you should only buy what you need or what you are definitely going to use. It reduces clutter and saves money. Trust me, I'm living, breathing proof.

My mum's kitchen (cough, it's actually mine) has every single baking bell and whistle. I even have a cake mixer that's a part-time oven. Nah, I'm only joking. I have a few cool things, though, but they've come with time, practice and seeing other great bakes that I want to try. Everything in good time. So, if you see yourself making loads of pastry, a food-processor might be a good idea. Don't get me wrong, making it by hand is great but they can be pretty handy, especially if you're short of time.

MY IDEAL KIT LIST

☆ a selection of baking tins – including 8cm moulds, 20cm cake tins, a 20–22cm fluted tart tin, a 23cm springform tin, 25cm cake tins, a 25cm springform tin, also 10cm tart tins, a 20 × 30cm high-lipped baking tray, a 21 × 30cm traybake tin, a 28 × 33cm tin and 2-litre pie dish

☆ a selection of cutters – including 5cm, 6cm, 7cm, 8cm, 10cm circle cutters, 5cm, 8cm and 10cm square cutters and ideally a crinkle-edged 5cm square cutter

☆ a free-standing mixer, hand-held mixer and a food-processor

☆ a whisk, rubber spatula, palette knife, long fish slice, wooden spoons and measuring spoons

☆ a selection of heatproof mixing bowls

☆ a turntable and cake leveller

☆ piping bags with a selection of nozzles (I use disposable bags)

☆ non-stick baking paper, silicone paper, clingfilm and kitchen paper

If you need any help with your baking just shout me on any of my socials – Instagram, Twitter – and I'll be there to help. Enjoy.

BIG LOVE,

LIAM x

BANANA CHOCOLATE SWISS

This was the first cake I made with Swiss meringue buttercream.
Even though it's more work, it is so worth the hassle, trust me. It's so much
creamier, silkier ... ahh, I could go on for ever.

SERVES 16-24

Banana Sponge

840g self-raising flour

½ tsp baking powder

1½ tsp ground cinnamon

½ tsp ground nutmeg

750g unsalted butter, softened

600g caster sugar

150g light brown sugar

12 large eggs

3 large bananas, mashed

180ml whole milk

1 tsp vanilla extract

Almond Swiss Buttercream

9 large egg whites

675g caster sugar

900g unsalted butter, softened
and cubed

½ tsp almond extract

Chocolate Mousse

150g dark chocolate (70% cocoa
solids), broken into chunks

½ tsp fine sea salt

50g caster sugar

4 large eggs, separated

150ml double cream

2 tbsp cocoa powder, sifted

Décor

100g dark chocolate (70% cocoa
solids), broken into chunks

100g almond flakes, toasted

a handful of banana chips

**You will need 4 × 25cm cake
tins**

Preheat oven to 180°C/Fan 160°C/
Gas 4. Grease and line the bases of the
cake tins.

> "OKAY SO, FIRST
> YOU WANT TO SET
> OUT ALL YOUR
> INGREDIENTS. TRUST
> ME, IT WILL MAKE
> YOUR LIFE SO MUCH
> EASIER."

CRACK ON WITH THE SPONGE

Sift your flour, baking powder, ground
cinnamon and nutmeg into a large bowl.

Cream your butter and both sugars
together in a large bowl with a free-
standing or hand-held mixer until light
and fluffy.

Crack the eggs in one at a time, mixing
after each addition. If the mixture begins
to curdle, just pop in a couple
of tablespoons of flour to bring it
back together.

Turn the speed down very low and add
your dry ingredients.

Finally, stir in your mashed bananas, then
loosen the cake mixture with your milk
and vanilla extract.

BAKE IT

Divide your mixture evenly between the
cake tins (see page 205) and bake for
25–30 minutes, or until a skewer inserted
into the middle comes out clean.

Remove from the oven and allow to
cool for 10–15 minutes in the tins before
turning out onto a wire rack.

SWISSING

Prepare a bain-marie (see page 205)
– this is just a saucepan with a few
centimetres of simmering water with
another bowl placed over the top. You
can use your free-standing mixer bowl
for this but make sure the water is not
touching the bottom of the bowl.

Add your egg whites to the bowl then
pour in your sugar. Place the bowl on
the saucepan and place the saucepan
over a low heat. Get your whisk and
begin to stir everything together until the
sugar has fully dissolved. The best way to
check this is to rub a bit of the mixture
between your fingers – if you can't feel
any sugar, it's ready.

Remove the bowl from the heat and,
using your whisk attachment in your free-
standing mixer or a hand-held whisk on
a medium to high speed, whisk for about
10 minutes, or until cool. You are aiming
for super fluffy clouds of meringue.

TURN OVER ⟶

Now it's time for decadence, add the butter chunks piece by piece and continue to whisk on a medium speed – take your time with this stage. Show your buttercream some love – the more patient you are adding the butter, the nicer your buttercream will be.

Before you know it, it'll be pretty much done. One more ingredient though – the almond extract. Pop that in and give it one more whisk for luck.

FOR YOUR CHOCOLATE MOUSSE

Measure your chocolate into a clean bowl and use your bain-marie to melt it, stirring occasionally. Add in your salt.

Meanwhile, measure the sugar into another bowl with the egg yolks and beat until smooth and silky.

Using a free-standing or hand-held mixer, whisk your egg whites in a large clean bowl until soft peaks are formed.

Finally, whisk the double cream in another bowl until it's at a "just-whipped" stage.

> "YOU ARE AIMING FOR SOFT PEAKS, SO YOU SHOULD BE ABLE TO HOLD THE BOWL UPSIDE-DOWN OVER YOUR HEAD – OOOOO RISKY!"

Add your cocoa powder to the egg yolks, then mix in the cream. Fold in the melted chocolate and finally tip in your whipped egg whites. Using a figure of eight motion, gently fold the egg whites into the chocolate mixture.

STACK 'EM

Use a cake leveller or sharp knife to trim the top off all the cakes so they are level.

Spread a small amount of buttercream on a board that is slightly bigger than your sponges and place your first layer of sponge on top. Place that board on a turntable, if you have one.

Fill two piping bags: one with half the Swiss buttercream and the other with the chocolate mousse. Cut the tip off both piping bags. While rotating the turntable, begin to pipe a buttercream border on the first layer of cake, leaving an 10cm circle in the middle. Fill that circle with a

third of the mousse filling, then place a layer of banana sponge on top. Repeat until all the sponges are stacked, making sure the final sponge is placed upside-down on top.

CRUMB COATING

Using a palette knife, cake scraper and a turntable, coat the sides and top of the cake with a thin layer of buttercream until it's covered. If you don't have a turntable, you can place your cake on a sturdy large board.

Place your cake in the fridge for at least an hour to set. Don't worry, it doesn't have to look spanking neat.

DÉCOR

Meanwhile, melt the chocolate using the bain-marie, stirring occasionally. Remove from the heat and leave to cool.

Place the other half of the Swiss buttercream in a piping bag with a round-tipped nozzle.

Take the cake out of the fridge and apply another layer of Swiss buttercream around and on top of the cake, using a palette knife to smooth the sides.

With the leftover buttercream, pipe around the edges of the cake.

Give the cake a good sprinkle of almond flakes and banana chips. Finally, take spoonfuls of the melted chocolate and squiggle lines all over the cake.

DONE DONE DONE! SLICE UP AND SERVE IT WITH A CUPPA. ENJOY BANANA SWISS!!

CHAI LATTE SWIRLS

Let's face it, I don't know anyone who doesn't like these. Go to any gran's house and you'll find, right at the back of the cupboard, the classic Mr Kipling's pack of six Viennese whirls. Okay, maybe not with a chai latte buttercream and chocolate hazelnut filling, but you get my point.

MAKES 20-25

Biscuit Dough

375g unsalted butter, softened
75g icing sugar
375g plain flour
75g cornflour
½ tsp ground cinnamon
1 tsp vanilla extract

Filling

125ml whole milk
3 tsp chai latte powder
150g unsalted butter, softened
300g icing sugar
½ tsp vanilla extract
100g chocolate hazelnut spread

Décor

icing sugar, to finish

Preheat oven to 190°C/Fan 170°C/Gas 5. Line 2 baking trays with baking paper.

DO THE DOUGH

Measure all the biscuit dough ingredients into a food-processor and pulse until combined and smooth. You may need to scrape down the sides of the bowl with a rubber spatula from time to time.

Spoon the dough into a piping bag fitted with a large star-tipped nozzle and pipe 6cm rosettes of the dough onto the prepared baking trays. You should be able to fit 20 to 25 biscuits.

TIME TO BAKE

Bake the biscuits for 15–17 minutes, or until pale golden brown.

Remove from the oven and leave on the baking tray for 5 minutes to firm up, then pop the biscuits onto a wire rack to finish cooling. Repeat with the leftover dough until you have 45 to 50 biscuits.

FOR THE FILLING

Pour your milk into a pan. Add the chai latte powder and place over a medium heat. Stir and bring just to the boil.

Remove from the heat and cool.

Measure the butter into a large bowl and, using a hand-held or free-standing mixer, beat until light and fluffy.

Sift your icing sugar into a separate bowl, then add to the butter in 3 stages, beating after each addition. Scrape down the sides of the bowl from time to time.

Add 1–2 tablespoons of the chai latte milk, along with the vanilla, to loosen the buttercream.

Spoon into a piping bag with a large star-tipped nozzle.

Measure the chocolate hazelnut spread into a heatproof bowl and melt in the microwave for 30 seconds or over a bain-marie (see page 205), to loosen. Pour this into another piping bag and snip the end.

SANDWICH THEM UP

Flip half the biscuits onto their backs and pipe buttercream rings around the edge of each biscuit, leaving a small circle in the middle. Now fill the middle with a chocolate hazelnut spread surprise!

Use your remaining biscuits to sandwich them up.

Finally, give each biscuit a light dusting of icing sugar.

"HERE'S A TRICK – GET A 6CM CUTTER AND DRAW AROUND IT ON TO THE BAKING PAPER TO MAKE 25 CIRCLES. WHEN YOU PLACE THE PAPER ON YOUR BAKING TRAY, FLIP IT OVER AND USE IT AS A GUIDE WHEN YOU ARE PIPING."

CHOCOLATE × ORANGE POLENTA CAKE

Two layers of orangey polenta cake with a coffee buttercream and a whipped dark chocolate filling. Oh, did I mention that it's gluten free, too?

SERVES 8–12

Orange Polenta Cake

250g unsalted butter, softened

250g caster sugar

4 large eggs

250g ground almonds

150g polenta

2 tsp gluten-free baking powder

zest of 3 oranges

2 tbsp orange juice

Coffee Buttercream

300g unsalted butter, softened

650g icing sugar

4 tbsp cold instant coffee

½ tsp vanilla extract

Ganache Filling

400ml double cream

300g dark chocolate (70% cocoa solids), broken into chunks

zest of 1 orange

Décor

50g candied orange peel, finely sliced

cocoa powder, to dust

You will need 2 × 20cm cake tins

Preheat oven to 160°C/Fan 140°C/Gas 3. Grease and line the cake tins with baking paper.

GET THE CAKE IN

Cream the butter and sugar together in a large bowl with a free-standing or hand-held mixer until light and fluffy.

Crack the eggs in one at a time, mixing after each addition. Add the almonds, polenta, baking powder, orange zest and juice and mix.

BAKE IT

Divide your mixture evenly between the cake tins and bake for 25–30 minutes, or until a skewer inserted into the middle comes out clean.

Remove from the oven and allow to cool for 10–15 minutes in the tins before turning out onto a wire rack.

BUTTERCREAM TIME

Measure your butter into a large bowl and beat with your free-standing or hand-held mixer until light and pale.

Sift your icing sugar into a separate bowl, then add it to the butter in 3 stages, beating after each addition.

Add your coffee and vanilla to loosen the buttercream and give it one more mix.

Spoon the buttercream into a piping bag and cut the tip off the end.

GANACHE

Pour your cream into a saucepan and place over a low heat. Bring to a gentle simmer.

Place the chocolate in a large bowl and pour the hot cream over the top. Leave to melt for a few minutes then add the zest and stir until it has a glossy and smooth consistency (see page 208).

Leave on one side to cool completely.

Once cool, use your whisk attachment in your free-standing mixture or hand-held whisk on a medium to high speed, to beat until light brown.

FILL × CRUMB COAT

Use a cake leveller or sharp knife to trim the top off both cakes so they are level.

Spread a small amount of buttercream on a board that is slightly bigger than your sponges and place your first layer of sponge on top. Place that board on a turntable, if you have one.

Place half the buttercream in a piping bag with a round-tipped nozzle. Pipe a buttercream border on the first layer of cake, leaving an 8cm circle in the middle. Fill the centre with your chocolate ganache, then place the second sponge upside down on top.

Using a palette knife, cake scraper and a turntable, coat the sides and top of the cake with a thin layer of the buttercream until it's covered. Place your cake in the fridge for at least an hour to set.

DÉCOR

Place the remaining buttercream in a piping bag. Apply another layer of buttercream around and on top of the cake. Smooth the sides with a palette knife, then pipe a circle of buttercream in the centre and fill it with buttercream kisses.

Decorate with some candied peel and give it a final dusting of cocoa powder.

OREO SHAKE CAKE

Well, where do I start? When I first discovered Oreo buttercream, my mind was blown. I literally used it with everything. Oh gosh, especially with a milkshake – and extra Oreos! The milkshake in the middle is optional but I tell you what, have a slice with a couple of slurps of the milkshake. Thank me later.

SERVES 16–24

Chocolate Sponge
825g caster sugar
780g plain flour
140g cocoa powder
1¼ tsp fine sea salt
2¼ tsp bicarbonate of soda
300g dark chocolate chips
525ml cold instant coffee
525ml buttermilk
480ml vegetable oil
8 large eggs

Oreo Buttercream
900g unsalted butter, softened
1.95kg icing sugar
150–180ml whole milk
2 × 154g packs Oreos

Chocolate Ganache
350ml double cream
200g dark chocolate (70% cocoa solids), broken into chunks

Décor
200ml double cream
6 ice cream wafers
2–3 tbsp chocolate flakes
a glass of milkshake (optional – see page 190 for a basic milkshake recipe)

You will need 4 × 25cm cake tins

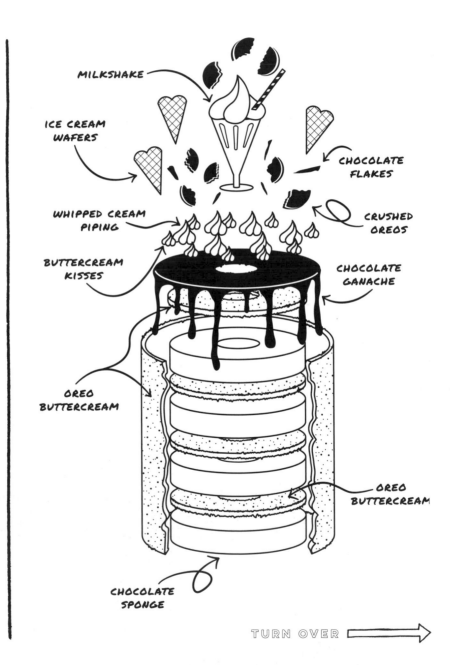

MILKSHAKE

ICE CREAM WAFERS

CHOCOLATE FLAKES

CRUSHED OREOS

WHIPPED CREAM PIPING

BUTTERCREAM KISSES

CHOCOLATE GANACHE

OREO BUTTERCREAM

OREO BUTTERCREAM

CHOCOLATE SPONGE

TURN OVER ⟹

MILKSHAKE IN THE MIDDLE OPTION: BEFORE YOU BEGIN THE CRUMB COAT, HOLLOW OUT YOUR SPONGES WITH A 10CM CUTTER – THIS IS TO ENSURE YOUR MILKSHAKE CAN FIT IN THE MIDDLE. POUR THE MILKSHAKE INTO A GLASS AND PLACE IN THE MIDDLE OF THE CAKE WHEN YOU ARE ADDING THE FINISHING TOUCHES.

Preheat oven to 180°C/160°C/Gas 4. Grease and line the cake tins with baking paper.

CRACK ON WITH YOUR SPONGE

Sift your sugar, flour, cocoa powder, salt and bicarbonate of soda into a large bowl. Add your chocolate chips.

Combine your coffee, buttermilk, vegetable oil and eggs in a separate bowl and give it a light whisk. Add the dry ingredients to the wet ingredients in 3 batches, mixing thoroughly after each addition.

Divide your mixture evenly between the cake tins and bake for 25–30 minutes, or until the sponges bounce back slightly when you press them gently.

Remove from the oven and allow to cool for 10–15 minutes in the tins before turning out on to a wire rack.

OREO BUTTERCREAM

Measure your butter into a large bowl and beat with your free-standing or hand-held mixer until light and pale.

Sift your icing sugar into a separate bowl, then add it to the butter in 3 stages, beating after each addition. Scrape down the sides of the bowl from time to time.

Add your milk to loosen the buttercream and give it one more mix.

Take 6 Oreos and break into pieces into a bowl. Set aside for décor later. Place the remaining Oreos in a plastic bag and, using a rolling pin, crush them to Oreo sand. You could use a food-processor, but that's just more washing up. Add the crushed-up Oreos to the buttercream and mix until it's all well incorporated.

FILL THEM UP

Use a cake leveller or sharp knife to trim the top off all the cakes so they are level.

Spread a small amount of buttercream on a board that is slightly bigger than your sponges and place your first layer of sponge on top. Place that board on a turntable, if you have one.

Fill a piping bag with half the buttercream and cut off the tip. While rotating the turntable, pipe buttercream on the first

layer of chocolate chip sponge then place another sponge on top. Repeat until all sponges are stacked, making sure your last sponge is placed upside down on top.

CRUMB COAT × SPECKLED EFFECT

Using a palette knife, cake scraper and a turntable, coat the sides and top of the cake with a thin layer of buttercream until it's covered. Place your cake in the fridge for at least an hour to set.

Fill another piping bag with the other half of the buttercream using a large nozzle of your choice.

Take the cake out of the fridge then apply another layer of buttercream around and on top of the cake using the palette knife to smooth the edges. Pop it back in the fridge.

MAKE YOUR GANACHE

Pour your cream into a saucepan and place over a low heat. Bring to a gentle simmer.

Place the chocolate in a large bowl and pour the hot cream over the top. Leave to melt for a few minutes then begin to stir with a wooden spoon, from the centre outwards, until it has a glossy and smooth consistency (see page 208).

> "DON'T TAKE TOO LONG BECAUSE YOU WANT THE GANACHE TO BE POURABLE."

DRIBBLE TIME!

When the ganache is just right, take the cake out of the fridge and spoon the ganache over the top edge, encouraging it to dribble down the sides. Fill in the middle of the cake with the leftover ganache.

DÉCOR

Whip your double cream in a large bowl to soft peaks, then fill a piping bag with a large star-tipped nozzle.

Use the remaining buttercream to pipe alternate kisses on top of your cake. Sprinkle over the Oreos pieces, stick some wafers in the top and scatter over the chocolate flakes.

CHEEKY DOUGHNUTS

Serious chosen one voice: The glazed.
Standard ring doughnut with the best glaze.
A true guilty pleasure!

MAKES 10

3 litres sunflower oil, for frying

Dough
500g strong white flour
60g caster sugar
10g fine sea salt
15g fresh yeast
150ml whole milk
4 large eggs
1 tsp vanilla extract
125g unsalted butter, softened

Glaze
500g icing sugar
150ml whole milk
150ml double cream
1 tsp vanilla extract

Décor (optional)
pistachios, chopped
freeze-dried strawberries
crumbled cookies
popcorn
cupcake sprinkles

You will need a free-standing mixer, 8cm and 3cm circle cutters, and a deep-fat fryer or food thermometer

This dough is pretty tricky to work with so I do think you need a free-standing mixer. If you don't have one, maybe you can borrow one from a loved one.

IT'S ALL ABOUT THE DOUGH

Put all the ingredients, apart from the butter, in the bowl of your mixer. Using the beater attachment, mix the dough on a medium speed for 10 minutes, until it forms a ball and comes away from the sides of the bowl.

Leave to rest for 5 minutes.

With the mixer on a medium speed, slowly add the butter about 20g at a time.

Once all the butter is incorporated, increase the speed to high for 5–7 minutes, until the dough is glossy and super elastic.

"YOU SHOULD BE ABLE TO STRETCH THE DOUGH FROM ONE SIDE OF YOUR KITCHEN TO THE OTHER – ONLY JOKING, DON'T TRY THAT!"

Cover the bowl with clingfilm and leave to prove at room temperature until it

has doubled in size – this takes around 3 hours.

Knock the dough back, then cover with clingfilm and put in the fridge to chill overnight.

THE NEXT DAY

Your dough should have doubled in size so knock it back again and roll it out on a lightly floured surface to a thickness of 1.5cm.

Using 8cm and 3cm circle cutters, begin to cut rings out of the dough. You may reroll the dough but, I'll warn you now, they won't be as good as the first batch.

Cut small squares of baking paper, slightly bigger than the doughnuts (so they have space to prove and expand) and place a ring on each one.

Lightly sprinkle all the doughnuts with flour, cover them loosely with clingfilm and leave to prove again for around 2 hours, until doubled in size. Check every hour or so – they will grow on you and you won't even realise.

TURN OVER ⟹

FRY UP

Pour your oil into a deep-fat fryer or large saucepan with a food thermometer (see page 205) and heat to 180°C. Line a tray with kitchen paper.

When deep-frying it's best to wear long sleeves to protect yourself from splashes and make sure kids are out of the way.

Carefully place 2 to 3 doughnuts in your fryer – don't worry about the baking paper, it will float off and you can easily take it out with some metal tongs. Fry the doughnuts on one side for 2 minutes, then flip and fry for 2 minutes on the other side.

Using your tongs, pick out your doughnuts and place them on the prepared tray.

Repeat this process until all your doughnuts are fried.

TIME FOR THE GLAZE

Sift your icing sugar into a large bowl and make a well in the centre. Add your milk, double cream and vanilla extract and begin to whisk until your glaze is thick.

> "IF THE GLAZE IS TOO THIN, ADD A LITTLE MORE ICING SUGAR AND WHIP THAT GLAZE LIKE YOU'VE NEVER WHIPPED ANYTHING BEFORE – THE DOUBLE CREAM WILL HELP TO THICKEN IT UP."

Dunk your doughnuts face down in the glaze and then remove with the tongs and place on a wire rack for the icing to set.

But wait – we're not done! Once all your doughnuts have been dipped, dip them again. Place back on the wire rack to set.

DÉCOR

Now get your toppings out! Scatter over some chopped pistachios, freeze-dried strawberries, crumbled cookies, popcorn or even cupcake sprinkles!

BUT IF YOU CAN'T WAIT, JUST START EATING 'EM! ONE DOUGHNUT PER PERSON ... OH, OK, MAYBE TWO ... AND A HALF!

WLB

White chocolate, lemon and blueberry: sweet ... tangy ... rich.
Nom nom nom nom. This is a combination that I love so much. Knock this
cake up for your pals, it will go down a storm.

SERVES 8-10

Sponge
225g unsalted butter, cubed
225g white chocolate, broken
into chunks
225g caster sugar
4 large eggs
225g self-raising flour
zest of 2 lemons
½ tsp vanilla extract

Blueberry Compote
300g frozen blueberries
1½ tbsp runny honey
7½ tbsp water
3 tbsp cornflour

White Chocolate
Buttercream
150g white chocolate, broken
into chunks
300g unsalted butter, softened
550g icing sugar
60ml whole milk
½ tsp vanilla extract

Garnish
10 lemon sweets

You will need a 900g loaf tin

Preheat oven to 180°C/Fan 160°C/Gas
4. Grease and line the loaf tin.

NOW FOR THE SPONGE

Melt the butter and white chocolate
in a heatproof bowl over a bain-marie,
stirring occasionally (see page 205).

Remove the bowl from the heat and
leave it to cool for a couple of minutes.

Using a hand-held or free-standing mixer,
beat in the sugar then add the eggs one
at a time.

Finally, fold in your flour, lemon zest and
vanilla extract.

Pour the cake mixture into the loaf tin
and bake on the middle shelf of the oven
for 1 hour.

Remove from the oven and allow to
cool for 10–15 minutes in the tin before
turning out onto a wire rack.

GET GOING ON THE BLUEBERRY COMPOTE

Tip your blueberries into a saucepan
with the honey and 1½ tablespoons of
the water.

In a small bowl, make a cornflour
paste by stirring the cornflour into the
remaining water. Add this paste to the
blueberries and cook them gently over a
low heat for 10–15 minutes until it has a
glossy, thick consistency – you want the

blueberries to hold their shape. Make
sure you taste as you go along and add a
little more honey if you like it sweeter.

Pour the blueberries into a bowl so they
cool down faster.

CRACK ON WITH YOUR BUTTERCREAM

Place the white chocolate in a heatproof
bowl set over a bain-marie. Allow to
melt, stirring occasionally.

Remove from the heat and set the bowl
aside to cool.

Measure your butter into a large bowl
and beat with your free-standing or
hand-held mixer until light and pale.

Sift your icing sugar into a separate bowl,
then add it to the butter in 3 stages,
beating after each addition. Scrape down
the sides of the bowl from time to time.

Add your milk and vanilla to loosen
the buttercream, then add your white
chocolate. Continue to beat on a slow
speed until thoroughly mixed.

TRIM × STACK

Using a cake leveller or sharp knife cut the cake into 3 layers horizontally.

Spread a small amount of buttercream on a rectangle display board and place your first layer of sponge on top.

Fill a piping bag with your buttercream and, using a round-tipped nozzle, pipe buttercream kisses on the sponge. Top with the second layer of sponge and repeat the buttercream process. Finally, top with the last layer of sponge.

Place the cake in the fridge for at least half an hour to set.

DRIZZLE-O-BLUE

Pipe buttercream kisses on the top layer. Then use your blueberry compote to drench that cake! Tip spoonfuls over the top and allow the juices to drip down the sides of the cake.

Finally, place the lemon sweets on top. Lovely!

TIN

There is no hiding that I'm a massive fan of playing with food. I always try to make everything as edible as possible. When I first started to bake, biscuits and cakes were my go-to bakes and, as always, I tried to combine them both. So, here it is – a biscuit-tin cake filled with their crunchy counterparts. Hey, fill the cake with whatever biscuits you like … I ain't judging.

SERVES 16–24

Ginger Cake

500g unsalted butter, softened
430g soft dark brown sugar
290g black treacle
50g runny honey
50g golden syrup
8 large eggs
500g self-raising flour
3 tbsp ground ginger
3 tsp ground cinnamon
1½ tsp ground cloves
5½ tbsp soured cream
10 pieces stem ginger (reserve syrup), finely chopped

Gingerbread

125g unsalted butter, cubed
100g dark muscovado sugar
3 tbsp golden syrup
1 tbsp black treacle
300g plain flour
1 tsp bicarbonate of soda
4 tsp ground ginger
½ tsp ground cloves

Speculoos Buttercream

600g unsalted butter, softened
1.3kg icing sugar
150ml whole milk
500g Speculoos spread
1½ tsp vanilla extract

Preheat oven to 190°C/Fan 170°C/Gas 5. Grease and line the cake tins with baking paper.

GET GOING ON THE CAKE

Cream your butter, sugar, treacle, honey and golden syrup together in a large bowl with a free-standing or hand-held mixer until pale.

Crack the eggs in one at a time, mixing after each addition.

Tip in your flour and spices and mix on a very slow speed – you don't want to overwork the mixture.

Once your dry ingredients are fully incorporated, stir in the soured cream and stem ginger.

Divide the mixture evenly between the cake tins and bake for 25 minutes, or until a skewer inserted into the middle comes out clean.

Remove from the oven and leave to cool in the tins.

CRANK UP YOUR OVEN FOR THE GINGERBREAD

Turn up the temperature to 200°C/Fan 180°C/Gas 6.

Measure the butter, sugar, golden syrup and treacle into a large saucepan and place over a medium heat to melt.

Sift your flour, bicarbonate of soda, ginger and cloves into a large bowl, then stir into the butter mixture to make a stiff dough. If the dough doesn't come together, add a splash of water.

ROLL × CUT × BAKE

Place a sheet of baking paper on your work surface and roll half the dough to the thickness of a £1 coin. Mark out a 18cm circle and remove the off-cuts. Slide the gingerbread circle, on its paper, on to a baking tray and bake for 15 minutes.

Place another sheet of baking paper on your work surface and roll out the remaining dough. Chomp out 4 × 5cm circles (these are going to make up the little knob for the biscuit lid) and use alphabet biscuit cutters to cut out the letters T I N.

Place all these pieces on their baking paper on to another baking tray and bake for 10 minutes.

TURN OVER FOR MORE INGREDIENTS ⟹

"IF I WAS YOU, I'D REROLL THE OFF-CUTS AND CUT OUT ANOTHER CIRCLE, JUST IN CASE THE FIRST ONE BREAKS, OR YOU HAVE A DOG OR ANNOYING NEPHEW WHO NIBBLES IT."

Royal Icing

1 large egg white
135g icing sugar
½ tsp glycerine
¾ tsp fresh lemon juice

You will need 4 × 20cm cake tins and a 10cm cutter

Remove all the gingerbread pieces from the oven and leave on the baking trays for 5 minutes to firm up, then place on a wire rack to finish cooling.

SPECULOOS BUTTERCREAM

Measure your butter into a large bowl and beat with your free-standing or hand-held mixer until light and pale.

Sift your icing sugar into a separate bowl, then add it to the butter in 3 stages, beating after each addition. Scrape down the sides of the bowl from time to time.

Add the milk to loosen the buttercream and give it one more mix, then stir in your Speculoos and vanilla.

ASSEMBLE TIME

Use a cake leveller or sharp knife to trim the top of all the cakes so they are level.

Cut out the centre of each sponge using a 10cm cutter.

Spread a small amount of buttercream on a board that is slightly bigger than your sponges and place your first layer of sponge on top. Place that board on a turntable, if you have one.

Fill a piping bag with half the buttercream, cut off the tip and, while rotating the turntable, begin to pipe buttercream on the first layer of cake. Place another layer of cake on top.

Repeat until all sponges are stacked, making sure your last sponge is placed upside down on top.

CRUMB COAT × TIN

Using a palette knife, cake scraper and a turntable, coat the sides and top of the cake with a thin layer of buttercream until it's covered. Give the inside of the cake a thin layer of buttercream as well. Place in the fridge for an hour to set.

Place the remaining buttercream in the piping bag and cover the cake with a final layer. Stick the letters TIN halfway up one side of the cake. Return to the fridge.

MAKE YOUR ROYAL ICING

Place the egg white in a large mixing bowl and whisk with a hand-held mixer until frothy.

Add the icing sugar a spoonful at a time, whisking after each addition.

Finally, add the glycerine and lemon juice and whisk until stiff peaks are formed. Too stiff? Add a little bit of water until you reach the desired consistency. Add a little icing sugar if it's too soft.

GINGERBREAD LID

Using some royal icing, stick one of the 5cm gingerbread rounds directly in the centre of the 18cm gingerbread circle.

Wait for this to dry, then attach another round. Repeat twice more so that you have 4 stacked rounds for a handle.

Leave the lid to set until ready to use.

REMEMBER IT'S A BISCUIT TIN

Take the cake out of the fridge and fill with any biscuits you like. Use the remaining royal icing to pipe whatever decorations you like on to the tin.

Pop the biscuit lid on top and enjoy with a cuppa.

NO, NO, NO, DON'T THROW AWAY THE OFF-CUTS – JUST HAVE THEM WITH SOME ICE CREAM. QUICK DESSERT, INNIT?

MEGA CHOCCY

Cupcakes were the first thing I made when I started baking. It's silly but, as much as everyone seems to make them, they'll always hold a special place in my sponge cake heart. I mean, let's be honest, the possibilities with them are endless. When the head of my sixth form saw the passion I had for baking, he asked me if I wanted to have my own cake sale. My pals and I called it "Cheeky Treats". We sold out and Mega Choccy was the bad boy that did it.

HAZELNUT SWITCH UP!! PUT A FERRERO ROCHER IN THE CENTRE OF EACH CUPCAKE, INSTEAD OF FILLING THEM WITH CHOCOLATE SAUCE, AND ADD 10 TABLESPOONS OF NUTELLA TO THE BUTTERCREAM.

MAKES 24

350g plain flour
370g caster sugar
55g cocoa powder
1 tsp bicarbonate of soda
½ tsp fine sea salt
150g dark chocolate chips
250ml buttermilk
250ml cold instant coffee
430ml vegetable oil
3 large eggs
1 tsp vanilla extract

Chocolate Sauce

100g dark chocolate (70% cocoa solids), broken into chunks
50g unsalted butter
300ml double cream
2 tbsp caster sugar
1 tsp vanilla extract

Buttercream

550g unsalted butter, softened
250g cocoa powder
850g icing sugar
150ml whole milk
½ tsp vanilla extract

You will need 2 × 12-hole muffin trays, 24 cupcake cases and an apple or cupcake corer

Preheat oven to 180°C/Fan 160°C/Gas 4 and line the muffin tins with cupcake cases.

MAKE IT × BAKE IT

Sift your flour, sugar, cocoa powder, bicarbonate of soda and salt into a large bowl. Add your dark chocolate chips.

Combine your buttermilk, coffee and veggie oil in a separate bowl and mix together.

Lightly beat your eggs in another bowl and add the vanilla. Tip the egg mixture into the coffee mixture and mix.

Add the dry ingredients to the wet ingredients in 3 batches, mixing thoroughly after each addition. Make sure it is mixed properly because you don't want any pockets of flour.

Divide your mixture evenly between the 24 cupcake cases and bake for 20–25 minutes, or until there's a spring back when you touch the sponges.

Remove from the oven and place the muffin tins on a wire rack to cool.

TOO MUCH SAUCE

Melt the chocolate and butter in a heatproof bowl set over a bain-marie or in the microwave, heating in 20-second bursts. Stir occasionally until it has completely melted.

Add all the other sauce ingredients and continue to stir until it's nice and smooth.

Remove from the heat and leave to cool.

TURN OVER ⟹

BUTTERCREAM TIME

Measure your butter into a large bowl and beat with your free-standing or hand-held mixer until light and pale.

Sift your cocoa powder and icing sugar into a separate bowl, then add it to the butter in 3 stages, beating after each addition. Scrape down the sides of the bowl from time to time.

Add the milk and vanilla extract to loosen the buttercream and give it one more mix.

> "THE BUTTERCREAM SHOULD BECOME LIGHTER IN COLOUR. IF IT IS STILL A BIT STIFF, ADD A COUPLE MORE SPLASHES OF MILK."

FILL EM UP × DÉCOR

Using an apple or cupcake corer, take the middle out of the cupcakes and fill with the chocolate sauce – all the way to the top.

Now I'm not going to tell you how to decorate these cupcakes because, in all fairness, there are so many ways to do it – pipe, dollop or swish with buttercream.

THE DODGING ZINGER

The thing about single-sided biscuits is, you can never just have one . . . so you might as well have two biscuits sandwiched together with a rosewater filling, lemon curd middle and pistachio crust. True? 'Ave a look . . .

MAKES 28-30

Biscuit Dough

290g plain flour, plus extra for dusting

½ tsp baking powder

½ tsp fine sea salt

180g unsalted butter, softened

150g golden caster sugar

1 large egg

1½ tsp vanilla extract

Crust

300g pistachios, shelled

5 tbsp dried rose petals, crushed

Filling

100g icing sugar

200g ricotta cheese

100g mascarpone cheese

100g Greek yoghurt

2 tbsp runny honey

1 tsp ground cardamom

¼ tsp rosewater

200ml double cream

340g lemon curd (shop-bought or see page 197)

You will need a 6cm cutter and a 2.5cm cutter

FOR THE BISCUITS

Measure the flour, baking powder and fine sea salt into a large bowl.

Place the butter in another large bowl and, using a hand-held or free-standing mixer with the beater attachment, beat for 1–2 minutes on a medium to high setting, until light and pale.

Add the sugar and beat again for roughly 2 minutes, until well creamed.

Finally, add the egg and vanilla, increase the speed and beat again.

> "DON'T FORGET TO SCRAPE DOWN THE SIDES OF THE BOWL AND GIVE IT ANOTHER MIX."

Add the dry ingredients to the butter mixture and mix on a low speed until well combined. Keep the speed low because you don't want to build up the gluten in the mixture or you'll get tough little lads. If the dough seems a bit soft, add an extra sprinkle of flour for better rolling consistency.

Divide the dough into two equal portions. Slightly flatten both balls of dough, wrap them in clingfilm and place in the fridge for at least an hour to chill.

Preheat oven to 180°C/Fan 160°C/Gas 4 and line two baking trays with baking paper.

ROLL × CHOMP × BAKE

Remove both slabs of dough from the fridge. On a lightly floured surface, roll each dough ball to the thickness of a £1 coin. Cut each one into circles using a 6cm cookie cutter.

Cut a 2.5cm circle out of the centre of half the biscuits.

You should have about 28–32 of each biscuit. Don't worry if you don't have that many – just make sure you have an equal number of each one.

Place the circles on one baking tray and the doughnut rings on another. Bake the rings for 10 minutes and the whole circles for 11 minutes, until a light golden brown. For an even colour, rotate the trays halfway through baking.

Remove from the oven and leave on the baking trays for 5 minutes to firm up, then place on a wire rack to finish cooling.

TURN OVER

CRUST

Bang your pistachios on to one of the used baking trays and toast them for 10 minutes in the oven (at the same temperature as the biscuits), giving them a quick stir halfway through.

Remove from the oven and set aside to cool.

Tip the nuts into a food-processor and blitz until a fine crumb – or just chop them up roughly instead.

Place in small bowl with the dried rose petals.

THE ROSE FILLING

Sift your icing sugar into a large bowl then, using a free-standing mixer or electric hand whisk, beat in your ricotta, mascarpone, yoghurt, honey, cardamom and rosewater until smooth. Add the double cream and whisk until it is a pipeable consistency.

ASSEMBLE TIME

Place the rose filling in one piping bag and the lemon curd in another. Snip the ends of both.

Turn all your circle biscuits on their backs and pipe a ring of rose filling around each edge. Dollop a little lemon curd in the middle. Finish off the sandwich by placing a ringed biscuit on top and gently press down.

Roll the edges of the biscuit sandwiches in the pistachio mixture. Repeat until all the biscuits are filled and covered.

FINESSED!

BAKLAVA ROLL UP

I'm from a place called Stoke Newington and we have a huge Turkish community there. I think that's where my love for Turkish food started. I grew an obsession for baklava – you only need the smallest piece to put a smile on your face. However, I have a few mates who think it is too sweet, so I thought it'd be a cool idea to take the flavour profile of baklava and try it in a different bake.

SERVES 8-10

Swiss Roll

6 large eggs

175g golden caster sugar, plus extra to dust

175g self-raising flour

finely grated zest of 1 orange

50g unsalted butter, melted and cooled

Filling

150g walnuts

150g pistachios, shelled

250g mascarpone cheese

250g full-fat cream cheese

75g icing sugar, sifted, plus extra to dust

½ tsp ground cardamom

2 tbsp runny honey, plus extra for drizzling

½ tsp orange blossom extract

100ml double cream

Décor

50g unsalted butter, melted

2 sheets filo pasty

You will need a 24 × 33cm Swiss roll tin

Preheat oven to 200°C/Fan 180°C/Gas 6. Line the Swiss roll tin and a large baking tray with baking paper.

MAKE IT × BAKE IT

Whisk the eggs and sugar together in a large bowl using an electric mixer, until light and fluffy.

Fold in the flour and orange zest.

"TAKE YOUR TIME WITH THE FOLDING – YOU DON'T WANT TO KNOCK ALL THE AIR OUT OF THE SPONGE."

Finally, fold in the butter.

Gently tip the cake mixture into the tin and bake for 15 minutes, or until pale but springy. Remove from the oven and leave in the tin to cool a little on a wire rack.

Meanwhile, place the sheets of pastry on the baking tray and brush lightly with melted butter. Bake for 15 minutes, then remove from the oven and leave to cool. Break them up into shards, ready to use.

Lightly dust a sheet of baking paper with golden caster sugar then turn out the cake on to the paper. Remove the paper from the base of the cake, then use the sugared paper to help roll it up. Leave it to cool.

NUTS

Tip the walnuts and pistachios into the used Swiss roll tin and roast in the oven for 15 minutes, stirring halfway through. Remove from the oven and leave to cool in the tin.

Blitz into a fine crumb using a food-processor, or chop finely by hand.

WHIP × SPREAD × ROLL

Measure the mascarpone, cream cheese, icing sugar, cardamom, honey and orange blossom extract into a large bowl and beat with an electric mixer until light and slightly thicker.

Add the double cream, then whisk again until it holds its shape.

Unroll the Swiss roll and spread a thin layer of the cream mixture on to the sponge, then sprinkle with half the nuts and a quarter of the filo pastry shards.

Reroll the sponge and place on a serving plate with the seam side down.

Dust with icing sugar, then add the remaining cream to a piping bag, and using a decorative nozzle pipe on top of the roll. Finish with the remaining nuts, pastry shards and a drizzle of honey.

VEGAN RED

"Red velvet is my favourite, but I'm a vegan now." Say no more …

SERVES 16–24

Red Velvet

500g plain flour

400g golden caster sugar

2 tsp bicarbonate of soda

1 tsp fine sea salt

2 tbsp cocoa powder

520ml vegan buttermilk (= 490ml vegan milk + 2 tbsp fresh lemon juice × mix and leave to sit for a couple of minutes)

4 tsp vanilla extract

150ml olive oil

2 tbsp apple cider vinegar

1 × 56ml bottle red food colouring

Buttercream

420g soya spread, chilled

1.3kg icing sugar

1 tsp vanilla extract

soya milk, to loosen

You will need 4 × 20cm cake tins

Preheat oven to 180°C/Fan 160°C/Gas 4 and grease the cake tins with soya spread and line with baking paper.

CRACK ON WITH YOUR SPONGES

Sift your flour, sugar, bicarbonate of soda, salt and cocoa powder into a large bowl.

Measure your buttermilk, vanilla, olive oil, vinegar and food colouring into a separate large bowl and mix.

Add the buttermilk mixture to the dry ingredients and whisk until there are no lumps whatsoever.

Divide the mixture evenly between the cake tins and bake for 25 minutes, or until a skewer inserted into the centre comes out clean.

Remove from the oven and allow to cool for 10–15 minutes in the tins before turning out onto a wire rack.

NOT-REALLY-BUTTERCREAM

Measure the spread into a large bowl and beat with a free-standing or hand-held mixer until pale.

Sift your icing sugar into a separate bowl, then add it to the spread in 3 batches, beating after each addition. Scrape down the sides of the bowl from time to time.

Add the vanilla to loosen the not-really-buttercream and give it another mix. If it still seems a little stiff, splash in some soya milk and give it one more mix.

CRUMB × FINAL COAT

Use a cake leveller or sharp knife to trim the top off all the cakes so they are level. Save the scraps for later.

Spread a small amount of buttercream on a board that is slightly bigger than your sponges and place your first layer of sponge on top. Place that board on a turntable, if you have one.

Fill a piping bag with half the buttercream, cut off the end and pipe buttercream on the first layer of sponge. Place another layer of cake on top. Repeat until all the sponges are stacked, making sure the final sponge is placed upside down on top.

Using a palette knife, cake scraper and a turntable, coat the sides and top of the cake with a thin layer of buttercream.

Place in the fridge for at least an hour to set.

Fill another piping bag with the other half of the buttercream, using a large nozzle of your choice. Apply another layer of buttercream to the sides and top of the cake, using the palette knife to smooth the edges. Use the remaining buttercream to decorate the cake as you wish.

Crumble the trimmed scraps of sponge and sprinkle over the cake.

"LEFTOVER
CHEESECAKE
CAN BE USED IN
YOU'RE TAKING
THE MICK, LIAM
(SEE PAGE 191)."

THIS CHEESECAKE HAS LEVELS

All right, this is it — if you want to flex your baking tekkers and you're a bit of a show off (we all are secretly), this cheesecake recipe is the one for you. Bring these little puddings to any dinner party or shindig and you'll shut it down — not with your dance moves but with your dessert.

SERVES 12

Macadamia Brown Butter Blondie

200g macadamia nuts

250g unsalted butter, cubed

420g light soft brown sugar

3 large eggs

1½ tbsp vanilla extract

330g plain flour

1½ tsp baking powder

1 tsp fine sea salt

Passion Fruit Cheesecake

900g full-fat cream cheese

230g caster sugar

95ml soured cream

3 large eggs

4 large egg yolks, lightly beaten

160g passionfruit pulp

1 tsp vanilla extract

Chocolate Bark × Cream

300g white chocolate, broken into chunks

finely grated zest of 2 limes

finely grated zest of 2 oranges

300ml double cream

2 tbsp caster sugar

2 tsp vanilla extract

You will need 12 × 8cm cylinder moulds, a 28 × 22cm baking tin and an 8cm cutter

Preheat oven to 200°C/Fan 180°C/Gas 6.

> "IF YOU DON'T HAVE CYLINDER MOULDS, GREASE AND LINE A 23CM SPRINGFORM TIN INSTEAD. YOU'LL NEED TO BAKE IT FOR AN HOUR AND LEAVE IT TO SIT IN THE OVEN FOR 50 MINUTES AFTER BAKING."

BROWNING BLONDIE

Scatter the nuts on a baking tray and roast in the oven for 10 minutes, tossing them halfway through.

Remove from the oven and leave on one side to cool.

Reduce the temperature to 180°C/Fan 160°C/Gas 4 and grease and line the baking tin.

BROWN THE BUTTER

Measure all the butter for the blondie into a saucepan and place over a medium heat until the milk solids have turned a deep amber colour and have almost burnt. Remove from the heat and pour into another bowl to cool.

Mix the sugar into the melted butter, then add the eggs one at a time, mixing after each addition, followed by the vanilla.

Tip in your flour, baking powder and salt and fold to combine. Finally, roughly chop the toasted macadamia nuts and stir them in.

Tip the mixture into the tin and spread evenly. Bake for 25–30 minutes, until golden brown.

> "YOU WANT YOUR BLONDIES TO BE SLIGHTLY FUDGY SO A SKEWER INSERTED INTO THE CENTRE SHOULD COME OUT SLIGHTLY WET."

Remove from the oven and leave in the tray until it's completely cool.

Reduce the oven temperature to 170°C/Fan 150°C/Gas 3.

TURN OVER ⟹

CRACK ON WITH THE CHEESECAKE

Measure your cream cheese and sugar into a large bowl and mix in your free-standing mixer with a paddle attachment on a medium speed or with a wooden spoon until smooth.

Add your soured cream and mix again until just combined.

Reduce the speed to medium-low and, while the machine is still running, add your eggs and yolks in a small stream. Mix thoroughly, then add the passionfruit pulp and vanilla, and combine gently.

CHOMP × FILL × BAKE

Cut 12 × 8cm circles out of the blondie and place a circle in each cylinder mould. Place all the moulds on a baking tray.

Divide the cheesecake mixture between the 12 moulds, filling them just to the top, and bake for 30 minutes, until the edges are set but the middle is slightly wobbly when the tray is shaken.

Turn off the oven but leave the cheesecakes inside with the door ajar for 30 minutes.

Remove from the oven and place on one side to cool completely.

Leave in the fridge to chill overnight.

NEXT DAY DÉCOR

Line a baking tray with baking paper.

Place the chocolate in a heatproof bowl set over a bain-marie (see page 205) or in a microwave, heating in 20-second bursts.

Pour the melted chocolate on to the baking tray and sprinkle with the lime and orange zests. Place in the fridge to set.

Whip the cream in a large bowl with the sugar and vanilla until soft-peak stage. Apply a dollop to every cheesecake to make it look like a soft cloud. Remove the cheesecakes from the cylinder moulds then break the chocolate slab into funky, pointy shapes and scatter over the top.

ACCEPT THE STACKING CHALLENGE AT YOUR OWN RISK!

NACH-O-ORDINARY TORTILLA CHIPS

Have you ever been indoors watching a film on — cough, cough — a very popular streaming service and fancied cinema-style nachos? Check it …

SERVES 8–10

3 litres vegetable oil, for frying

Chocolate Sauce

100g dark chocolate (70% cocoa solids), broken into chunks

50g unsalted butter

250ml double cream

2 tbsp caster sugar

1 tsp vanilla extract

Cinnamon Sugar Popcorn Tortilla Chips

100g salted popcorn

100g caster sugar

½ tsp ground cinnamon

15 corn tortillas, each sliced into 8 triangles

Lime Cream Cheese Dollop

150g soured cream

150g full-fat cream cheese

2 tbsp runny honey

zest of 2 limes

juice of 1 lime

a few small mint leaves

Décor

1 × punnet strawberries, washed, sliced and cubed

You will need a deep-fat fryer or food thermometer

GET GOING ON YOUR CHOCOLATE SAUCE

Melt the chocolate in a heatproof bowl over a bain-marie (see page 205) or in the microwave, heating in 20-second bursts, stirring occasionally until it has completely melted.

Tip all the other ingredients for the sauce into another saucepan and place over a gentle heat. Stir until the butter has melted and the sugar has dissolved then stir this into the melted chocolate.

Remove from the heat and leave on one side to cool.

TORTILLA CHIPS

Blitz your popcorn in a food-processor to a fine crumb.

Place the sugar and cinnamon in another bowl then tip in the popcorn crumbs.

Pour your oil into a deep-fat fryer or large saucepan and, using a food thermometer, heat to 180°C (see page 205).

When deep-frying it's best to wear long sleeves to protect yourself from splashes and make sure kids are out of the way.

> "IF YOU ARE USING A LARGE SAUCEPAN, BE CAREFUL AND KEEP AN EYE ON IT."

Deep-fry the corn triangles for 1 minute until golden, crisp and brown. Remove using tongs.

Drain on kitchen paper then toss into the cinnamon popcorn sugar mix.

DOLLOP × DÉCOR

Mix your soured cream, cream cheese, honey and the zest and juice of 1 lime in a bowl then plop this into a small serving dish. Finish with the zest of another lime and a few small mint leaves.

Place your tortilla chips in a massive serving bowl and put the bowl of dollop in the middle.

Scatter the strawberries over the top of the chips and pile on the chocolate sauce.

Get stuck in!

SAVOURY
....

OI, OI, FULL BREKKY FOR TWO

Everyone loves a good old full English breakfast – eggs, bacon, beans, the lot – but sometimes you don't want the crazy portions. So, here's a cheeky hack and, trust me, you won't be missing out on anything.

SERVES 2

Soda Bread

125g plain flour, plus extra for dusting

125g plain wholemeal flour

½ tsp bicarbonate of soda

1 tsp fine sea salt

200ml buttermilk

4 tbsp mixed seeds

Brekky

vegetable oil, for greasing

50g cherry tomatoes, roughly chopped

20g baby spinach, roughly chopped

30g chestnut mushrooms, thinly sliced

4 rashers of cooked bacon or 100g smoked salmon

4 large eggs

fine sea salt, to taste

cracked black pepper, to taste

You will need 2 × 14cm round pie dishes

Preheat oven to 200°C/Fan 180°C/Gas 6 and line a baking tray with baking paper.

SODA BREAD

Measure both flours, bicarbonate of soda and salt into a large bowl and mix well.

Make a well in the centre and pour in about half the buttermilk. Encourage the flour into the buttermilk using your hands.

___

"HANDS ARE THE ONLY WAY TO GO."

___

Continue to add the buttermilk until the flour has absorbed all of it.

Tip the dough on to a lightly floured surface, knead in the mixed seeds then shape into a ball and slightly flatten it.

___

"BUD, YOU HAVE TO MOVE QUICK COS THE BUTTERMILK IS ALREADY REACTING WITH THE BICARB – CHOP, CHOP, CRACK ON."

___

Put the dough on the baking tray, mark a deep cross into the top of the dough with a large, sharp knife and make sure the cut is deep. You should be flirting with almost cutting through, that's how deep the slashes need to be.

Dust the top with flour and bake for 20–25 minutes, until golden brown. Tap the base of the loaf, if it sounds hollow it's ready.

Leave to cool slightly on a wire rack.

MAKE YOUR BREKKY

Turn up your oven to its highest setting and lightly grease two pie dishes with a little oil.

Divide the tomatoes, spinach, mushrooms and bacon or salmon between your two pie dishes.

Crack 2 eggs into each one and season both with salt and pepper.

Pop the dishes in the oven (at the same temperature as the bread) for 10 minutes – you want the egg whites to be set but the yolks should still be slightly runny.

Serve immediately with the soda bread.

FALAFEL SCONES

Okay, ask any of my pals, whenever we go out – morning, noon or night – there isn't a time when I don't fancy a falafel wrap. With the whole savoury scone craze, I've wondered for a while what a falafel-inspired scone would taste like. Hmmmmm …?

MAKES ABOUT 30

Chickpea Crumb

1 × 400g tin chickpeas, drained
1 tsp rapeseed oil
1 tsp smoked paprika
1 tsp ground cumin
1 tsp ground turmeric
1 tsp dried mixed herbs

Scone

720g plain flour, plus extra for dusting
3 tbsp baking powder
½ tsp fine sea salt
200g unsalted butter, cold, cubed
a small bunch of chives, snipped
a small bunch of parsley, leaves picked and chopped
300g feta, diced
15 halves of sun-dried tomatoes, diced
4 large eggs
160ml whole milk

You will need a 6cm cutter

Preheat oven to 180°C/Fan 160°C/Gas 4.

CHICKPEA CRUMB

Chuck the chickpeas into a large bowl with all the other ingredients and mix until the chickpeas are well coated.

Tip on to a baking tray and bake for 16 minutes. Rotate the tray and bake for a further 16 minutes. Leave on one side to cool.

Drop the temperature to 170°C/Fan 150°C/Gas 3 and line a baking tray with baking paper.

FOR THE SCONES

Sift your flour, baking powder and salt into a large bowl.

Add your butter and, using your fingertips, rub the butter into the flour until there are no clumps left.

> ## "YOU'RE AIMING FOR A COARSE BREADCRUMB TEXTURE."

Stir in the fresh herbs and mix until evenly distributed.

Finally, add the feta and sun-dried tomatoes and stir again.

Crack 3 of the eggs into a jug with the milk and beat lightly. Pour this into the bowl, stirring as you go. Bring the mixture together to form a rough dough.

> ## "TRY NOT TO OVERMIX THE DOUGH OR YOUR SCONES WILL COME OUT TOUGH.. YOU WANT FALAFEL SCONES NOT STONES!"

Dust your worktop and rolling pin with flour then roll your dough into a 25 × 25cm square about 3–4cm thick.

Dip a 6cm cutter into flour then cut out about 18 scones. You want to use one swift motion when cutting, they say it helps the scones to rise. Re-roll the off-cuts of dough and cut out more scones until you have a dozen. Place them on the baking tray.

GLAZE × CRUMB

Beat the remaining egg and, using a pastry brush, slather the top of your scones with the egg wash.

Finally, blitz the cooled chickpeas in a food-processor to a fine crumb and sprinkle this over the scones.

Bake for 20–25 minutes until well risen. The base should be a deep, golden brown and they should sound hollow when tapped.

CHEESY GARLIC MONKEY

My guilty pleasure, well, one of many, is garlic bread – especially when it has loads of cheese and the garlic swings in and lingers there … Yum. Balls of cheesy garlicky goodness – perfect for a dinner party or just for a casual catch up with pals. You know what you should try this with? BBQ sauce – it's banging, trust me.

SERVES 6-8

Herb Butter

1 garlic clove, minced

125g unsalted butter, softened

a handful of thyme, leaves picked and finely chopped

a handful of parsley, leaves picked and finely chopped

a small bunch of chives, snipped

fine sea salt, to taste

Dough

175ml whole milk

2 tsp golden caster sugar

100g unsalted butter, cubed, plus extra for greasing

500g strong white bread flour

1 tsp fine sea salt

7g fast-action dried yeast

2 tbsp fresh basil, chopped

2 tbsp fresh oregano

4 large eggs, lightly beaten

300g Cheddar, grated

You will need a 25cm springform cake tin

HERB BUTTER

Place all the herb butter ingredients in a large bowl and beat with a hand-held mixer to combine.

Tip on to some baking paper or clingfilm, roll and wrap up, then place in the fridge until needed.

DOUGH

Warm the milk in a saucepan over a gentle heat.

Remove from the heat and stir in the sugar and butter. Keep stirring until the butter has melted. Allow to cool to lukewarm.

Sift your flour and salt into a large bowl, stir in the yeast and herbs then make a well in the centre. Pour in your beaten eggs and lukewarm milk and give it a quick mix to form a soft pillowy dough.

Knead by hand for 15 minutes, until elastic, super soft and sticky.

LET IT SLEEP

Pop the dough in a lightly oiled bowl, cover with some oiled clingfilm and leave for 1½–2 hours, until doubled in size.

Lightly brush the cake tin with melted butter.

KNOCK × ROLL × FILL

Knock back the dough and sprinkle half the grated cheese over the top. Knead for 1–2 minutes, until the cheese is well distributed.

Divide the dough into 19 equal-sized balls. (Weigh each ball – you're aiming for 50g balls. If the balls are different sizes, the bread won't cook evenly.)

Pinch each ball underneath like a balloon and roll to make a smooth ball. Arrange them in concentric circles around the tin.

Sprinkle half the remaining cheese in the gaps between the balls, cover again and leave to prove for a further 2 hours, until well risen.

Preheat oven to 200°C/Fan 180°C/Gas 6.

BAKE YOUR BREAD

Bake your bread for 30–35 minutes.

Meanwhile, melt the herb butter in a small pan over a low heat.

Remove the bread from the oven and brush your buns with the herb butter and sprinkle over the remaining cheese.

Pop back in the oven and bake for a further 10 minutes, until golden.

Make sure you serve it warm – the cheeeeese neeeeds to ooooooze.

COOL BEANS

It's a phrase that I pretty much say all the time, so why not
make it into a recipe? A spicy bean and pumpkin chilli topped with
good old pastry. Shout out to my vegetarian massive!

SERVES 6

**Spicy Bean and Pumpkin
Chilli Filling**

3 tbsp olive oil

1 onion, diced

1 red onion, diced

3 garlic cloves, minced

1 Scotch bonnet chilli, seeded
and finely chopped

1½ tsp cayenne pepper

1 tsp oregano

2 tsp dried mixed herbs

2 tsp smoked paprika

700g pumpkin or butternut
squash, peeled and cut into
cubes

100g black olives

160ml red wine

1 × 400g tin chopped tomatoes

½ vegetable stock cube

1 × 230g jar piquillo pimiento
peppers, drained and roughly
chopped

1 × 400g tin black beans, drained
and rinsed

½ × 400g tin pinto beans,
drained and rinsed

Pastry

525g plain flour, plus extra for
dusting

1 tsp fine sea salt

135g unsalted butter, cold, cubed

135g lard, chilled, cubed

4½ tbsp cold water

1 large egg, beaten

**You will need a 2-litre
ovenproof dish, at least 4cm
deep with a wide rim**

CHILLI TIME

Place a large, heavy-based frying pan
with a lid over a medium heat. Add the
oil, onions and garlic and cook, stirring
occasionally, until softened.

Stir in the chilli, herbs and spices and
cook for 2 minutes or so.

Tip in the squash, olives and wine. Leave
to simmer for a couple of minutes.

Stir in the tomatoes and 200ml water.
Crumble in the stock, stir and bring to a
gentle simmer. Cover with a lid and cook
for 30–35 minutes, stirring occasionally.

> "FLAVOUR UPON
> FLAVOUR, THE
> LONGER IT SIMMERS
> THE BETTER IT'S
> GONNA TASTE ...
> THIS FILLING IS
> NUTS!"

Add the peppers, taste for seasoning
and, if it looks a little dry, add some more
water. Cook for a further 25 minutes
until the pumpkin is tender.

> "SOMETHING
> MISSING? SEASON
> UP YOUR CHILLI –
> ADD AS MUCH AS
> YOU LIKE."

Finally, add both your beans, taste for
seasoning. Pour into your ovenproof dish.
Leave to cool.

Mix the chives into the soured cream
and place in a small bowl.

PASTRY PARTY

Sift your flour and salt into a food-
processor. Add the butter and lard and
pulse until it resembles fine breadcrumbs.

Add the water on a running motor until
it comes together to form a rough ball.

Tip on to a lightly floured surface and
gently knead until smooth.

Roll the pastry out on a lightly floured
surface until it is about 2.5cm larger than
the top of the pie dish.

Cut a thin strip around the edge of
the pastry, brush it with some beaten
egg then press it on to the rim of the
pie dish. Brush this with a little more
egg then gently lift the pastry on top.
Press the edges together to seal, trim
any excess pastry and crimp the edges
between your fingers.

Brush the top with beaten egg, then chill
for 30 minutes.

Preheat oven to 220°C/Fan 200°C/Gas 7.

Bake the pie for 30 minutes then serve
up to family and friends.

PIE 'N' PLAY V.1

Two guilty pleasures in one. I will always have time for video games …
even when I have loads of uni work to do. (Yes, sometimes my priorities
can be questionable.) These pies are what this book is all about:
combining bakes with everyday life.

SERVES 4

Sweet Potato and Chorizo Filling

750g sweet potatoes, peeled and cubed

3 tsp smoked paprika

30g light brown sugar

½–1 tsp fine sea salt

cracked black pepper, to taste

2 tsp ground cinnamon

4 tbsp olive oil

2 tbsp vegetable oil

2 red onions, chopped

2 spring onions, chopped

12 cherry tomatoes, halved

100g sun-dried tomatoes, chopped

2 tbsp dried mixed herbs

1 large chorizo sausage, skinned and chopped

2 handfuls of spinach

300g feta, crumbled

Pastry

700g plain flour, plus extra for dusting

1 tsp fine sea salt

400g unsalted butter, cold, cubed

3 large eggs

2 tbsp cold water

You will need 4 × 16cm pie dishes

Preheat oven to 200°C/Fan 180°C/ Gas 6.

SWEET POTATO TIME

Place your sweet potatoes in a large bowl and season with the smoked paprika, sugar, salt, pepper and cinnamon.

Add the olive oil and toss everything together to coat the cubes.

Tip into a baking tray and roast for 35 minutes, until tender.

LET'S MAKE THE PASTRY

Tip the flour, salt and butter into your food-processor and pulse until it resembles fine breadcrumbs.

Crack 2 of the eggs into a bowl with the cold water and beat lightly.

While the motor is running, add the egg and water mixture and pulse until it starts to come together into a ball.

Tip the pastry on to a lightly floured work surface and gently bring it together.

Divide the dough into a quarter and three-quarters. Wrap both balls in clingfilm and place in the fridge to chill.

CHORIZO FRY UP

Place a large frying pan over a medium heat and add the vegetable oil.

When hot, toss in your red and spring onions, your cherry and sun-dried tomatoes, and your dried mixed herbs. Cook until they have softened, then add your chorizo sausage and cook for a further 6–8 minutes.

Remove from the heat and stir in your spinach. Leave it to wilt.

FILLING FINALE

Combine your sweet potatoes and the chorizo mixture in a large bowl, sprinkle over your feta and stir carefully.

ROLL × LINE × FILL

Place two baking trays in the oven to heat up.

Get your large piece of pastry out of the fridge and roll out on a lightly floured surface into a large rectangle the thickness of a £1 coin. This is going to be the base for all your pies. Cut the dough into quarters and place each rectangle into a pie tin. Gently encourage the pastry into the corners of the tins.

TURN OVER ⟶

Trim the pastry edges off your pies and begin to fill them up. Don't worry if you have filling left over; just leave it to cool and place it in an airtight container – it'll be ready for the next pies you make!

Take the small piece of pastry out of the fridge and roll it out on a lightly floured surface. Cut 4 rectangles slightly larger than the top of the pies.

Beat the remaining egg in a small bowl to use as an egg wash. Brush pastry around the edge of the rectangles and place the lids on top. Crimp the edges of each pie with the back of a fork to seal, then egg wash the top of all four pies.

GAMES CONTROLLERS × BAKE

Re-roll the off-cuts of pastry and cut to make the components of 4 game controller consoles.

Give the pies a final egg wash, making sure you cover the areas where there are grooves on your pastry. Place on the preheated trays in the oven and bake for 25–30 minutes, until golden brown.

Remove from the oven and place on a wire rack to cool for a few minutes before serving because the filling will be piping hot.

THIS PIE IS IMMENSE WITH GRAVY. I MEAN, ANY PIE IS GREAT WITH GRAVY. TRUE?

TAKEOUT ROLL UP

The classic sausage roll × famous spring roll = BAM!!

SERVES 6

2 tbsp sesame or sunflower oil

1 small onion, diced

3 spring onions, finely chopped

1 tbsp snipped chives

200g beansprouts, rinsed and dried

1 garlic clove, minced

1cm piece fresh root ginger, peeled and grated

2 tbsp oyster sauce

2 tbsp dark soy sauce

2 tbsp Hoisin sauce

juice and zest of 1 lime

100g breadcrumbs

100g pork mince

400g pork sausages, skinned

3 sheets filo pastry

100g unsalted butter, melted

1 large egg, beaten

4 tbsp sesame seeds

fine sea salt, to taste

cracked black pepper, to taste

Bonus recipe: Sweet × Sour Sauce

1 tbsp cornflour

1 tbsp water

170ml pineapple juice

80ml rice vinegar

65g light brown sugar

3 tbsp ketchup

1 tbsp soy sauce

1 tbsp sesame or sunflower oil

1 large onion, diced

1 green pepper, diced

1 × 230g tin pineapple chunks

Preheat oven to 200°C/Fan 180°C/Gas 6 and line a large baking tray with baking paper.

FRY UP

Place a large non-stick pan over a medium heat and add a couple of splashes of oil. Add the onions, chives and beansprouts, and gently fry until softened and golden.

Measure the garlic, ginger, oyster, dark soy and Hoisin sauces into a bowl, along with the zest and the juice of the lime and give it a good stir.

Add to the pan and cook for a further 2–3 minutes.

Tip into a large bowl and add the breadcrumbs. Give it a good stir, then season well and set aside to cool.

MAKE THE SAUSAGE

Once cool, add the pork mince and sausage meat to the breadcrumb mixture and mix well.

"OI, DON'T YOU DARE MIX IT WITH A SPOON! GET YOUR HANDS STUCK IN, MATE. HERE'S A TRICK – IT'S BEST IF YOUR HANDS ARE SLIGHTLY WET."

Roll the mixture into a 25cm sausage – you can pop the filling in clingfilm and give it a good roll to get an even, compact shape. Set aside.

PASTRY TIME

Place one of the sheets of pastry on your work surface with the shortest end closest to you and brush lightly with some melted butter. Place the second sheet on top, but slightly off-centre, 6cm to the right to be exact, and brush again with a little more butter. Finally, top with the final sheet. The final rectangle of pastry should be roughly 40 × 45cm.

TURN OVER ⟹

SAUSAGE FORMATION

Place your sausage meat across the pastry – removing the clingfilm if you've used it. There should be an 8cm border of pastry around the sausage.

Fold up the bottom of the pastry, it should start to cover the filling, then fold in the sides, gently but firmly. Now roll the pastry from the bottom to the top to wrap the filling.

"TAKE YOUR TIME, IT'S YOUR LITTLE SAUSAGE BABY."

Place on the baking tray, give it a good egg wash with the beaten egg, then sprinkle with some sesame seeds.

Bake for 30 minutes, until the filling is cooked and the pastry is golden brown.

BONUS RECIPE: SWEET × SOUR SAUCE

Whisk the cornflour and water together in a small bowl and set on one side.

Place the pineapple juice, rice vinegar, sugar, ketchup and soy sauce in a saucepan over a medium heat and bring to the boil.

Stir in your cornflour mixture and cook for 2 minutes to thicken.

Meanwhile, place a frying pan over a medium heat and add a couple splashes of oil. Chuck in your onions and peppers and cook until soft.

Finally, add your pineapple and, when your fruit has heated through, add to your sauce.

SERVE UP

Cut your roll into hefty chunks and serve with your sauce.

TAKEAWAY WHO? OH, OKAY, YOU CAN ORDER IN SOME PRAWN CRACKERS OR DUMPLINGS BUT, STILL, YOU KNOW WHAT I'M ON ABOUT – ENJOY!

"PUT THAT PHONE DOWN! NO PIZZA DELIVERY NEEDED HERE."

WHEEL UP THE PIZZA

Pizza … one of my all-time favourites. Just to step it up a notch,
how about 12 whirls slathered with a banging tomato sauce, with a healthy
amount of cheese. You know what I mean by "healthy", right?

SERVES 6

Dough

450g strong white bread flour,
plus extra for dusting

7g fast-action dried yeast

2 tsp golden caster sugar

1 tsp fine sea salt

2 tbsp olive oil

300ml warm water

Filling

150g pesto

24 pepperoni slices

250g sun-dried tomatoes,
drained and roughly chopped

80g black olives, pitted, thinly
sliced

Tomato Sauce

2 tbsp olive oil

2 garlic cloves, minced

2 sprigs of thyme, leaves picked

a handful of basil leaves, plus
extra to finish

2 × 400g tins plum tomatoes

fine sea salt, to taste

cracked black pepper, to taste

Topping

150g mozzarella, grated

150g Cheddar, grated

Bonus Dip

300g soured cream

300g crème fraîche

2 garlic cloves, minced

juice of 2 lemons

4 tbsp snipped chives

**You will need a 25cm
springform tin**

IT'S ALL ABOUT THE DOUGH

Measure the flour, yeast, sugar and salt into a large mixing bowl, or the bowl of your free-standing mixer.

Add the olive oil and warm water and start to give it a good mix until it forms a dough. Use the dough attachment if you have a mixer.

Knead the dough on a lightly floured surface for about 10 minutes, or for 5 minutes on medium speed in your mixer with a dough hook attachment.

> "HERE'S A TIP – YOUR DOUGH IS READY WHEN IT FEELS SOFT, SPRINGY AND ELASTIC."

Clean your bowl, squiggle in a couple tablespoons of olive oil and pop the dough back in. Cover with some oiled clingfilm and leave in a warm place for 1–3 hours, until doubled in size.

FREE PUNCHING BAG

Line the base of the tin and grease the sides.

Uncover the dough and knock all the air out of it. Tip on to a lightly floured surface, give it a sprinkle of flour just in case the dough is sticky, and roll out to a 40 × 30cm rectangle.

Spread the pesto evenly on top of the dough, then scatter over the pepperoni, tomatoes and olives.

ASSEMBLE

Roll up the dough from one of the long sides into a long sausage.

Using a sharp knife, cut the sausage into 12 equal pieces, then place each swirl face up on the springform tin, making sure the end of each roll is tucked in towards the centre of the arrangement.

> "UNROLLING DURING COOKING IS A NO GO."

Leave a little space between each swirl as they will grow during the last prove. Cover with some more oiled clingfilm and leave to prove for 30–60 minutes, until almost doubled in size.

Preheat oven to 200°C/Fan 180°C/Gas 6.

TURN OVER ⟹

CRACK ON WITH THE SAUCE

Place a large frying pan over a medium heat and pour in a generous amount of olive oil and allow it to heat up.

Add the garlic and cook until golden brown.

Immediately, stir in your thyme, basil and plum tomatoes and give your tomatoes a squash.

Season with salt and pepper to taste, then bring up to a boil.

Remove from the heat and pass the sauce through a sieve to get rid of the lumps. Return the sauce to the pan and bring back to a boil.

Turn down the heat and leave to simmer gently for 5–10 minutes.

Remove from the heat and place in a separate bowl to cool.

PIZZA TIME

Once the dough has doubled in size, bake for 35 minutes, until golden brown.

Remove from the oven and leave to cool on a wire rack.

"IS IT FINISHED? NAH!"

Spread a couple of ladlefuls of pizza sauce on the dough, then make it rain with both grated cheeses and pop it back in the oven for a further 10 minutes, until the cheese is bubbly gold and … yum.

Remove from the oven, scatter some basil leaves on top and squiggle with olive oil.

BONUS RECIPE – THE DIP

Tip the soured cream, crème fraîche, garlic and lemon juice in a food-processor and blitz until the ingredients are thoroughly mixed. Tip into a small bowl and stir in the chives.

"WE ALL KNOW YOU HAVE TO HAVE DIPS WITH YOUR PIZZA, RIGHT?"

SPAGURROS

We all know them, we all love them, but one thing I will say is that there are hardly any savoury versions of this sweet treat … until now. This is what would happen if churros asked a bowl of spaghetti bolognese to be friends.

MAKES ABOUT 30 CHURROS

2 litres sunflower oil, for frying

Bolognese Dipping Sauce

2 tbsp olive oil

2 onions, minced

2 carrots, peeled and finely chopped

3 garlic cloves, minced

2 sprigs of thyme, leaves picked and chopped

2 sprigs of rosemary, leaves picked and chopped

500g beef mince

1 × 400g tin plum tomatoes

a small bunch of basil, leaves picked and chopped

3 bay leaves

pinch of dried mixed herbs

3 tbsp tomato purée

125ml beef stock

fine sea salt, to taste

cracked black pepper, to taste

Savoury Churros

75g unsalted butter, melted

375g plain flour

1½ tsp baking powder

1 tsp fine sea salt

2 tbsp dried mixed herbs

To Finish

1 × 180g bag lightly salted tortilla chips, blitzed into crumbs

100g Parmesan, finely grated

You will need a deep-fat fryer or food thermometer

FRYING × BROWNING

Place the olive oil in a large frying pan over a medium heat.

Chuck in your onions, carrots, garlic, thyme and rosemary and fry for 10 minutes, stirring until the veg has softened.

Whack up the heat to medium-high, add the mince and fry for 5 minutes, until the meat has browned all over.

SAUCING IT UP

Add the tomatoes, basil, bay leaves, mixed herbs, tomato purée and beef stock, along with some salt and pepper to taste. Continue to stir until the tomatoes have broken up.

Bring the sauce to a boil then turn down the heat, cover with a lid and leave to simmer gently for 1–1¼ hours, making sure you stir occasionally, until it becomes an insanely rich, thick sauce.

PARMESAN CHURROS

Boil the kettle and measure 525ml of boiling water into a jug, then add the melted butter.

Sift your flour, baking powder, salt and mixed herbs into a large mixing bowl and make a well in the centre.

Pour in the liquid from the jug and quickly beat the water into the flour with a wooden spoon until there are no lumps.

Leave the dough to rest for 20 minutes.

FRY × COAT

Fit a large piping bag with a 1–2cm star-tipped nozzle and fill with the dough. Line a baking tray with kitchen paper and place the crushed chips in a wide bowl.

Pour your oil into a deep-fat fryer or large saucepan with a food thermometer and heat to 190°C (see page 205).

> "COOKING WITH OIL CAN BE EXTREMELY DANGEROUS, SO BE CAREFUL."

Pipe 3 strips of dough approximately 8cm long directly into the pan, snipping the ends with scissors. Fry for 2–3 minutes until golden brown and super crisp. Make sure the churros are roughly the same length, so the cooking time is the same.

TURN OVER ⟶

THEY CALL
ME THE
CHURROS
MAN.

"I NEED TO WARN YOU
THAT CHURROS COULD
EXPLODE, SO MAKE SURE
YOU ARE WEARING LONG
SLEEVES WHEN FRYING.
ALSO MAKE SURE ANY
KIDS ARE OUT OF THE WAY.
THEY CAN COME BACK
INTO THE KITCHEN TO
TOSS THE CHURROS IN THE
CRISP COATING LATER."

Remove the churros using a slotted spoon or tongs and place them on the lined baking tray.

Crack on until all the churros are cooked.

Toss the drained churros in the crushed-up crisps then pop them on a massive serving dish. Scoop ladlefuls of your spagbol sauce into a bowl and place it in the middle of the churros. Finish with a sprinkling of Parmesan ... Voilà!

PATTIE QUICHE

My mum, my sister and I have some weird habits, including a slight obsession with quiche. To make it even worse, we used to have baked beans and chips with it! No greenery, just golden food. The local Caribbean restaurant makes patties with a pastry that is somewhere between a shortcrust and a rough puff with a sort of flaky texture kind of thing and I love it. So, combining two of my loves – quiche and traditional Caribbean patties – we have the Pattie Quiche!

MAKES 8

Pastry

800g plain flour, plus extra for dusting

4 tsp ground turmeric

2 tsp curry powder

1 tsp fine sea salt

500g unsalted butter, frozen

250ml cold water

Salmon

520g skinless salmon fillet

2 garlic cloves, minced

2 tbsp dry mixed herbs

2 tbsp fresh dill, chopped

juice of 1 lemon

fine sea salt, to taste

cracked black pepper, to taste

Filling

1 tbsp light olive oil

1 onion, roughly chopped

1 red onion, roughly chopped

10 cherry tomatoes

a large bunch of spinach

10 large eggs, beaten

200ml whole milk

400ml double cream

fine sea salt, to taste

cracked black pepper, to taste

a few sprigs of thyme, leaves picked

You will need 8 × 12cm tart tins

Preheat oven to 190°C/Fan 170°C/Gas 5.

FOR THE PASTRY

Place the flour in a large bowl and stir in the turmeric, curry powder and salt.

Grate the butter into the bowl and lightly toss it around with a table knife to coat it in the flour.

Add the water slowly, stirring constantly until it comes together and forms a dough. Bring it together into a ball, wrap in clingfilm and place in the fridge to chill.

SEASON YOUR SALMON

Place your salmon in foil and season with the garlic, mixed herbs, dill, lemon juice and salt and pepper.

Bake for about 20 minutes, until the salmon is just about to start falling apart.

Turn the oven temperature up to 200°C/Fan 180°C/Gas 6 and place two baking trays in to heat up.

SORT YOUR FILLING

Place a pan over a medium heat and add the oil, both your onions and tomatoes and cook until the onions are tender.

Pop in your spinach to wilt then break your salmon into flakes and chuck it into the pan.

Meanwhile, crack your eggs into a large bowl and give them a light whisk. Pour in the milk and cream and mix again. Season with salt, pepper and thyme, keeping some leaves to garnish.

ROLL × FILL × BAKE

Divide the pastry into 8 and roll each piece out on a lightly floured surface to a thickness of £1 coin. Line your tins with your pastry, leaving an overhang. Prick the bases with a fork, top with a square of baking paper and fill each one with baking beans.

Place the tins on the heated baking trays and blind bake for 15–17 minutes.

Remove from the oven and drop the temperature to 160°C/Fan 140°C/Gas 3.

Discard the paper and baking beans and divide the salmon mixture evenly between the pastry cases.

Pour over the egg filling, sprinkle with thyme and bake for 20–30 minutes.

Remove from oven and allow to cool to set further.

Trim the quiches' pastry overhang and serve them with anything.

"ACTUALLY, TRIMMING IS OPTIONAL. INCONSISTENCY IS ART! LET THE QUICHES HAVE THEIR OWN IDENTITY ... YES, I AM A DRAMA STUDENT!"

SHOUT OUT TO NAN

You already know, Nan's curried goat in a pie, enough said.

SERVES 4

1kg diced leg of goat, lamb or mutton

juice of 1 lemon

3 garlic cloves, crushed

50g fresh root ginger, peeled and grated

2 tbsp mild curry powder

2 tsp ground turmeric

4 tsp all-purpose seasoning

2 sprigs of thyme, leaves picked

1 onion, chopped

1 red onion, roughly chopped

1 yellow pepper, roughly chopped

1 red pepper, roughly chopped

knob of unsalted butter

2 large potatoes, peeled and roughly chopped

1 Scotch bonnet pepper, roughly chopped (optional)

2 ripe plantains

2 tbsp vegetable oil

Pastry

700g plain flour, plus extra for dusting

2 tsp ground turmeric

1 tsp fine sea salt

400g unsalted butter, cold, cubed

3 large eggs

2 tbsp cold water

SEASON UP A DAY AHEAD

Tip your meat into a large bowl and fill the bowl with cold water. Squeeze the lemon over the top and leave it to sit for a couple of minutes.

Drain the meat well and return to the dry bowl. Add the garlic, ginger, curry powder, turmeric, all-purpose seasoning, thyme, both onions and peppers, and give the meat a good massage with your hands until everything is evenly distributed.

Cover the bowl in clingfilm and pop in the fridge overnight.

> "THE QUANTITIES I'VE GIVEN FOR YOUR SEASONINGS ARE JUST A GUIDE. TEMPTED TO ADD EXTRA CURRY POWDER? THEN SLAP IT IN THERE! GO WITH YOUR FLAVOUR INSTINCTS."

TIME TO COOK

Tip all your meat into a large pot, add a cheeky knob of butter and a splash of water and cover with a lid. Place over a medium heat and bring to the boil.

Turn the heat down and leave to cook gently over a low heat for 1 hour until tender – or longer if you have the time.

> "YOU WANT THE MEAT TO BE TENDER. LOW AND SLOW, THAT'S WHAT THEY SAY, INNIT?"

Add your potatoes and the Scotch bonnet pepper, if using, and cook for a bit longer.

PLANTAIN FRY

Meanwhile, cut the plantains into 1cm slices, then place a large frying pan over a medium heat and add the oil. Fry the plantains on both sides until crisp golden brown.

Remove from the pan and place on kitchen paper to absorb the excess oil.

> YOU NEED BODY FOR THIS PIE AND MAYBE A BIT OF SPICE IF YOU DARE.

TURN OVER FOR MORE INGREDIENTS ⟶

Salsa

1 large mango, peeled and diced

2 avocados, peeled and diced

100g pomegranate seeds

125g goats' cheese, crumbled

1 red onion, diced

grated zest and juice of 2 limes

2 tbsp olive oil

a small bunch of coriander, finely chopped

You will need 4 × 16cm pie dishes

PASTRY TIME

Tip the flour, turmeric, salt and butter into a food-processor and pulse until it resembles fine breadcrumbs.

Crack 2 of the eggs into a bowl with the cold water and beat lightly.

While the motor is running, add the egg and water mixture and pulse until it starts to come together.

Tip the pastry on to a lightly floured work surface and gently bring it together. Divide the dough roughly into a quarter and three-quarters and wrap both balls in clingfilm. Place in the fridge to chill.

Preheat oven to 200°C/Fan 180°C/Gas 6 and place two baking trays in the oven.

LINE YOUR PIES

Get your large piece of pastry out of the fridge and roll out on a lightly floured surface into a large rectangle the thickness of a £1 coin. This is going to be the base for all your pies. Cut the dough into quarters and place each rectangle into a pie tin. Gently encourage the pastry into the corners of the tins.

Trim the pastry edges off your pies then place a thin layer of plantain on to the base of each pie. Finally, fill with the curried goat.

LIDS × BAKE

Take the small piece of pastry out of the fridge and roll it out on a lightly floured surface. Cut 4 rectangles slightly larger than the top of the pies.

Beat the remaining egg and brush the egg wash around the edge of the rectangles and place the lids on top. Crimp the edges of each pie with the back of a fork to seal, then egg wash the top of all four pies. Cut small slits in the centre of each lid.

Place the pies on the preheated baking trays and bake for 20–25 minutes.

Remove from the oven and place on a wire rack to cool slightly before serving because the filling will be piping hot.

SALSA × SERVE

Meanwhile, combine all the salsa ingredients in a large bowl, give it a good mix and serve it alongside your pies.

"THERE WILL BE LEFTOVER CURRY, NO DOUBT. BUT IT'S A FAMILY TRADITION TO HAVE LEFTOVERS FOR MONDAY'S DINNER, AND I WANT YOU LOT TO BE A PART OF THAT AS WELL."

SALT FISH DOUGHNUTS

Caribbean takeaway restaurants are well known for selling filled fried dumplings. The filling can vary from jerk chicken, pumpkin and chana to curried goat but, as much as I love dumplings (my nan's are the best), sometimes you want a lighter kind of dough to cuddle that amazing filling. So here it is …

MAKES ABOUT 16

3 litres vegetable oil, for frying

Turmeric Dough

500g strong white flour, plus extra for dusting

2 tsp ground turmeric

50g caster sugar

10g salt

15g fresh yeast

75ml water

75ml whole milk

4 large eggs

1 tbsp tamarind paste

125g unsalted butter, softened

Salt Fish Filling

8 fillets salt fish

2 bunches of callaloo, stems removed

2 tbsp vegetable oil

2 large onions, roughly chopped

2 large peppers (red × yellow), roughly chopped

2 tomatoes, roughly chopped

black pepper, to taste

fine sea salt, to taste

You will need free-standing mixer and a deep-fat fryer or food thermometer

This dough is pretty tricky to work with so I do think you need a free-standing mixer. If you don't have one, maybe you can borrow one?

DOUGH A DAY AHEAD

Put all the ingredients, apart from the butter, into a free-standing mixer and, using the beater attachment, mix on medium speed for 10 minutes, until it forms a ball and comes away from the sides of the bowl.

Leave the dough to rest for 5 minutes.

Slowly add the butter, about 20g at a time, with the mixer on medium speed.

Once all the butter is incorporated, increase the speed to high and beat for 5–7 minutes, until the dough is glossy and super elastic.

Cover the bowl with clingfilm and leave to prove until doubled in size.

Knock back the dough then return to the bowl, cover with clingfilm again and put in the fridge to chill overnight.

Place your salt fish in a large bowl, cover in cold water and leave to soak overnight.

COOK YOUR FILLING

Drain your salt fish and place in a large saucepan. Cover with fresh water, place over a medium heat and bring to the boil. Let it bubble away for 30 minutes.

> "MAKE SURE YOU DO THIS STEP – TRUST ME, SALT FISH CAN BE INCREDIBLY SALTY."

Meanwhile, place your callaloo in a bowl of cold water and leave to soak for 10 minutes.

Drain the fish and place on one side.

Place a large frying pan over a medium heat and add the oil.

Break your fish into small chunks and tip into the pan. Cook for 5–10 minutes.

Drain the callaloo and add it to the pan with the remaining ingredients and continue to cook until the onions are tender.

Remove from the heat and place in a bowl on one side.

> "GOOD OL' CALLALOO IS THE COUSIN OF SPINACH – IT'S SUPER TASTY, GOOD FOR YOU AND EXTREMELY VERSATILE. IF YOU CAN'T GET HOLD OF IT YOU ARE ALLOWED TO USE SPINACH … JUST THIS ONCE THOUGH."

TURN OVER

WAKE UP YOUR DOUGH

Your dough should have doubled in size so knock it back again and roll out on a lightly floured surface into 50g balls.

"WEIGH THEM, DON'T EYE BALL THEM. I MEAN, I'D BE TEMPTED TO GUESS AS WELL BUT DON'T!"

Put each ball on a square of baking paper, slightly bigger than the ball, so it has space to prove and expand.

Lightly sprinkle all the balls with flour, cover with clingfilm, and leave to double in size. Check them every hour or so – they'll grow on you and you won't even realise.

NOW IT'S TIME FOR FRYING

Pour your oil into a deep-fat fryer or large saucepan with a food thermometer and heat to 180°C (see page 205). Line a baking tray with kitchen paper to absorb the excess oil.

When deep-frying it's best to wear long sleeves to protect yourself from splashes and make sure kids are out of the way.

Carefully place 2 to 3 doughnuts in your fryer at a time and fry on the first side for 2 minutes. Flip with metal tongs or two wooden dowels and cook on the other side.

"DON'T WORRY ABOUT THE BAKING PAPER – ONCE THE DOUGHNUTS START FRYING, THEY'LL FLOAT OFF AND YOU CAN TAKE THEM OUT WITH YOUR METAL TONGS."

Remove your doughnuts from the oil and place them on the prepared tray.

Repeat this process until all your doughnuts are fried.

FILL 'EM UP

Taking one doughnut at a time, cut halfway down and fill with the salt fish.

TOP UP WITH SOME SALAD, FRIED PLANTAIN OR TAMARIND SAUCE.

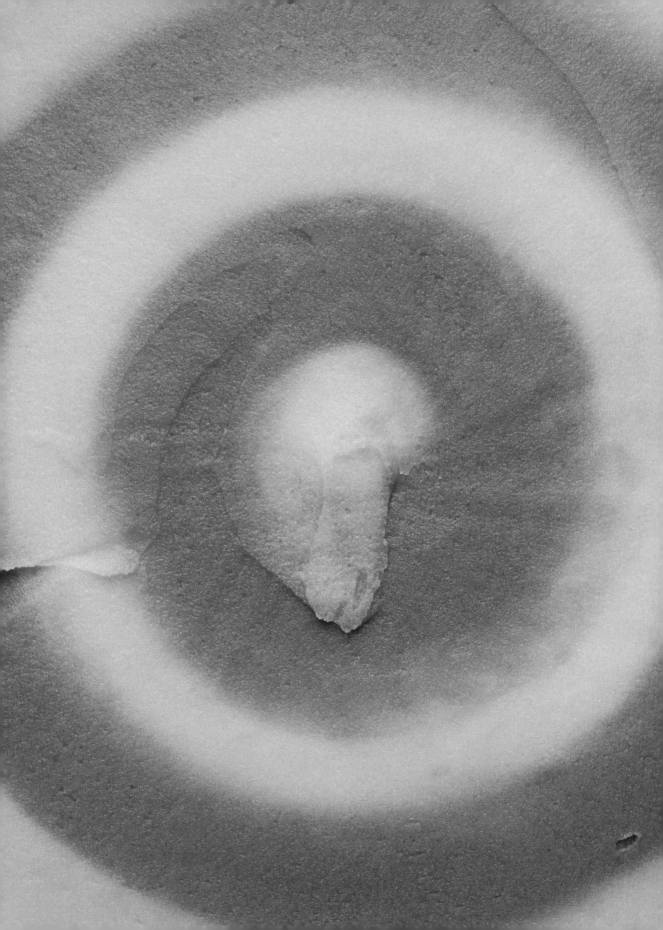

Nostalgia

BUN × CHEESE

Around Easter time, it's safe to say every Caribbean household stocks up on mixed spice dried fruit loaf served with all the cheese you like. Go for good mature melted cheese. Crazy!!

MAKES 24

600g strong white flour, plus extra for dusting

10g fine sea salt

45g caster sugar

2 tsp ground cinnamon

a grating of nutmeg

½ tsp ground cloves

230ml stout

100ml water

1 tbsp gravy browning

½ tsp vanilla extract

22g fresh yeast

1 tbsp treacle

1 tbsp runny honey

100g unsalted butter, softened

150g raisins

50g plain flour

1 large egg, beaten, for glaze

Line two baking trays with baking paper.

DOUGH TIME

Measure your flour, salt, sugar and all the spices into a large bowl and mix well.

Pour your stout, water, gravy browning, vanilla and yeast into another bowl and whisk until the yeast has dissolved.

Add the water mixture into the flour, with the treacle and honey, and mix with a free-standing mixer on a medium speed for 8–10 minutes, or mix well with a wooden spoon, until the dough comes away from the sides.

Sprinkle a little extra flour over the dough and leave to rest for 20 minutes.

Slowly add the butter, about 20g at a time, with the mixer on medium speed or kneading by hand.

Once all the butter is incorporated, add your raisins then increase the speed to high and beat for a further 2 minutes, or knead by hand for around 5 minutes, until the dough is glossy and elastic.

PROVE IT

Divide the dough into 50g balls (weigh each ball to make sure they are evenly sized) and place them on the baking tray. Cover loosely with clingfilm and leave for 1–2 hours, until doubled in size and slightly joined together.

BAKE THE ROLLS

Preheat oven to 200°C/Fan 180°C/Gas 6.

Mix the flour with enough water to make a thick paste, then spoon into a piping bag and cut off the end. Pipe crosses on top of the buns, then give the tops a good brush with beaten egg. Bake for about 15 minutes, until the bases of the buns are light golden brown.

Remove from the oven and place on a wire rack to cool.

SPLIT 'EM, ADD A GOOD KNOB OF BUTTER AND A SLAB OF CHEESE, MAYBE A BIT OF PICKLE – THE POSSIBILITIES ARE ENDLESS.

BREAKFAST!! OH, WAIT ... CUPCAKES!!

Let's be honest, as much as we might not want to admit it, breakfast cereals play
a massive part in our lives, especially when we are young. Those primary school
days when mums and dads are trying to feed us wholesome porridge, maybe
sneaking fruit on top, but all we crave are the silly sweet cereals. I had a favourite
and I was only allowed to eat it on Fridays. Here's an ode to my favourite
childhood cereal. Who would have thought using breakfast cereal
milk could be so amazing? Thank you, Christina Tosi.

MAKES 24

Breakfast Milk – Night Before

150g your favourite cereal

1.1 litres whole milk

50g light brown sugar

generous pinch of salt

Sponge

330g unsalted butter, softened

330g caster sugar

6 large eggs

330g self-raising flour

1½ tsp baking powder

90ml Breakfast Milk

½ tsp vanilla extract

Cereal Custard Filling

750ml Breakfast Milk

1 tsp vanilla extract

150g caster sugar

6 large egg yolks

60g cornflour

60g unsalted butter

Preheat oven to 170°C/Fan 150°C/Gas 3
and line a baking tray with baking paper.

BREAKFAST FOR DINNER

Spread your favourite cereal on the tray
and toast in the oven for 15–20 minutes.

Place on one side to cool.

Tip the cooled cereal into a large bowl
and pour your milk over the top. Stir
then leave the milk to steep for 30
minutes at room temperature.

Strain the milk through a sieve, discarding
the cereal and collecting the milk in a
medium-sized bowl. Use the back of a
ladle to gently press down on the cereal
in the sieve to get all the flavour out.

Stir your sugar and salt into the milk and
give it a good whisk.

Store in an airtight container ready for
tomorrow.

Preheat oven to 180°C/Fan 160°C/
Gas 4 and line the muffin trays with
cupcake cases.

RISE AND SPONGE

Cream your butter and sugar together
in a large bowl with a free-standing or
hand-held mixer until light and fluffy.

Crack the eggs in one at a time, mixing
after each addition.

Sift your flour and baking powder into a
separate bowl then add to your butter
mixture with the speed turned down
very low.

Finally, add the Breakfast Milk and vanilla
to loosen the mixture.

Divide the mixture evenly between
the cupcake cases and bake for
22–25 minutes, or until a skewer
inserted into the middle comes
out clean.

Remove from the oven and place both
trays on a wire rack to cool.

TURN OVER FOR MORE INGREDIENTS

Buttercream

600g unsalted butter, softened

1.3kg icing sugar

120ml Breakfast Milk

1 tsp vanilla extract

100g your favourite cereal, crushed

To Finish

your favourite cereal

chocolate spoons (optional)

You will need an apple or cupcake corer, 2 × 12-hole muffin trays and 24 cupcake cases

CEREAL CUSTARD FILLING

Place a saucepan over a medium heat and add the Breakfast Milk and vanilla. Bring to the boil then take off the heat.

Meanwhile, whisk the sugar, egg yolks and cornflour together in a large bowl.

Pour a little of the milk into the sugar mixture, constantly whisking, then whisk in the remaining hot milk, pouring it in a steady stream until it is well combined.

Pour the custard back into the saucepan and place over a gentle heat, keep stirring until the custard becomes very thick.

Remove from the heat and pass the custard through a sieve.

Add the butter and stir until melted.

Pop a sheet of clingfilm on the surface of the custard to stop a skin from forming and set aside.

BUTTERCREAM

Measure your butter into a large bowl and beat with your free-standing or hand-held mixer until light and pale.

Sift your icing sugar into a separate bowl, then add it to the butter in 3 stages, beating after each addition.

Add your Breakfast Milk and vanilla to loosen the buttercream and give it one more mix.

Finally, add your crushed cereal and give it one more stir. BAM! Cereal buttercream.

"IF THE BUTTERCREAM IS A LITTLE STIFF, ADD A SPLASH MORE BREAKFAST MILK AND GIVE IT A GOOD MIX. BREAKFAST IS ALMOST READY."

TO FINISH

Using an apple or cupcake corer, take the centre out of each cupcake and fill with the custard.

Place the buttercream in a piping bag and, using a round-tipped nozzle, pipe two rings of buttercream around the top of each cupcake. It's a buttercream bowl! But with no cereal … so fill each hole with your favourite cereal and serve it with a chocolate spoon, if you like.

BREAKFAST IS DONE!

PACKED LUNCH

In primary school, apart from maths, lunch was my favourite part of
the day, especially when it was packed lunch. I never knew what sandwich I would
be getting. Re-creating my love for sandwiches in biscuit form.

MAKES 15 SANDWICHES

Biscuits

340g unsalted butter, softened

165g golden caster sugar

340g plain flour, plus extra for dusting

165g cornflour

1 tsp fine sea salt

Ribena Buttercream

200g unsalted butter, softened

400g icing sugar

4 tbsp Ribena

1 tsp vanilla extract

Topping

200g milk chocolate, broken into chunks

icing sugar, to dust

200g Classic Smooth (see page 199) or shop-bought smooth peanut butter

BISCUIT TIME

Cream your butter and sugar together in a large bowl with a free-standing or hand-held mixer until light and fluffy.

Sift your flour and cornflour into a separate bowl, add the salt and mix together.

Add the dry ingredients to the butter mixture and mix until smooth.

Tip the dough on to a lightly floured surface and begin to knead – but don't go crazy – until it forms a soft dough.

Cut the dough in half, wrap both halves in clingfilm and leave to chill in the fridge for 20 minutes.

BUTTERCREAM UP

Measure your butter into a large bowl and beat with your free-standing or hand-held mixer until light and pale.

Sift your icing sugar into a separate bowl, then add it to the butter in 3 stages, beating after each addition. Scrape down the sides of the bowl from time to time.

Take a couple of tablespoons of the Ribena and add to the bowl along with the vanilla to loosen the buttercream.

Cover the bowl with clingfilm and set aside until needed.

Preheat oven to 180°C/Fan 160°C/ Gas 4 and line two baking trays with baking paper.

BAKE IT

Remove the dough from the fridge and roll it out on a lightly floured surface until 1cm thick.

Cut as many 8cm squares as you can, then cut these squares in half to form two triangles. These will act as your "bread".

Reroll any off-cuts until all the biscuit dough is finished – or you could save it for another day by wrapping in clingfilm and leaving in the fridge.

Place your triangles on the baking trays and bake for 20 minutes, until a light golden brown colour.

Remove from the oven and leave on the trays for 5 minutes to firm up, then transfer to a wire rack to cool.

TURN OVER

PACKED LUNCH

Place the chocolate in a heatproof bowl set over a bain-marie (see page 205) or in the microwave, heating in 20-second bursts.

Pour the chocolate on to a plate and gently smooth out.

Remove the biscuits from their cooling racks and cover the racks in baking paper.

Pick up each biscuit and dip two edges into the melted chocolate then return to the cooling rack.

"THIS WILL ACT AS YOUR CRUST."

Once they are all covered, pop them in the fridge to set.

Dust a small plate with icing sugar.

Dip the chocolate-covered sides of the biscuits into the icing sugar and return to the cooling rack.

"THIS IS YOUR FLOUR."

FILL ∗ SANDWICH

Melt the peanut butter in a small saucepan over a gentle heat, until slightly runny.

Tip into a piping bag. Spoon the ribena buttercream into another piping bag. Snip both ends.

Turn half of the biscuits on to their backs and pipe a triangle of buttercream around the edges, leaving a small gap in the middle – make sure you don't go too close to the edge, though, as it will ooze.

Fill each gap with the warm peanut butter then top with another biscuit.

CARROT CAKE COOKIES

I was in the sixth form when one of my teachers asked me to make
her a carrot cake. I went through a phase of making complementary biscuits
to go with cakes I baked, so these carrot cake cookies were made.
Since then I've developed the recipe and these cookies are not anyone's
sidekick any more … Carrot Cake Cookies take centre stage.

MAKES 15

Filling

150g full-fat cream cheese
150g icing sugar
1 tsp vanilla extract

Dough

350g plain flour
½ tsp baking powder
1 tsp ground cinnamon
1 tsp mixed spice
1 tsp ground cloves
150g unsalted butter, softened
100g soft light brown sugar
50g soft dark brown sugar
1 large egg
200g carrot, finely grated

Décor

zest of 2 oranges and juice of
1 orange
4 tbsp walnuts, finely chopped

FILLING × DOUGH

Mix the cream cheese, 3 tablespoons of
the icing sugar and the vanilla in a large
bowl until combined, then pop in the
freezer for 30–45 minutes.

Meanwhile, measure your flour, baking
powder and spices into another bowl.

Beat your butter and both sugars
together in a third bowl until creamy.

Beat your egg into the butter mixture,
then tip in your carrot. Mix together well.

Tip your dry ingredients into the carrot
mixture and mix slowly to form a dough.

ROLL × FILL

Preheat oven to 200°C/Fan 180°C/Gas 6.

Line a baking tray with baking paper.

"FLOUR YOUR HANDS!"

Weigh your dough and divide by 15 –
this is how much each ball should weigh.
Then flatten them slightly into thin discs
using the palm of your hand.

Add a generous teaspoon of the cream
cheese filling to the centre of each disc
and wrap the dough around the filling to
seal. Pinch the top and roll it back into a
ball, making sure no filling leaks out.

Pop the balls on to the tray and flatten
slightly. Place in the fridge to chill for
30 minutes.

BAKE

Bake the cookies for 20 minutes, until
golden brown.

Remove from the oven and leave on the
tray for a few minutes to firm up, then
transfer to a wire rack to cool further.

DÉCOR

Sift the remaining icing sugar into a small
bowl and mix with the orange juice –
you're aiming for a drizzling consistency.

Flick the icing over the cookies and top
with the orange zest and walnuts.

"THESE ARE BEST EATEN THE
DAY THEY'RE MADE. THEY'LL
KEEP FOR UP TO 2 DAYS IN AN
AIRTIGHT CONTAINER. POP THEM
IN THE FRIDGE THOUGH – DAIRY
IN THE MIDDLE, INNIT."

TART PBJ

Sounds like a mouthful, doesn't it? Whenever I am coming up with new recipes, I always try to think of new flavour combinations, whether they work or not … Hmm, let's just say the baked bean and custard combo didn't work. But this one does, so have a go!

SERVES 8

Pastry

260g plain flour, plus extra for dusting

130g unsalted butter, cold, cubed

zest of 2 lemons

2 sprigs of thyme

1 large egg yolk

2 tbsp icing sugar

2 tbsp cold water

Filling

100g Honey Nut Roasted (see page 199) or shop-bought peanut butter

80g plain flour

1 tsp baking powder

120g unsalted butter, softened

150g golden caster sugar

1 large egg white

50g blackberry jam

100g honey-roasted peanuts, roughly chopped

Topping

5 tbsp icing sugar

2 tbsp blackberry jam

a handful of honey-roasted peanuts, roughly chopped

You will need a 20–22cm fluted tart tin

START THE PASTRY

Tip the flour, butter, lemon zest and thyme into a food-processor and pulse until it resembles fine breadcrumbs.

While the motor is running, add the egg yolk, icing sugar and water until it starts to clump together.

Tip on to a lightly floured surface and give the pastry a quick knead to bring it together. Flatten into a thick disc, wrap in clingfilm and place in the fridge to chill for 30 minutes.

MAKE THE FILLING

Add all the ingredients, apart from the jam and peanuts, to the food-processor and blitz until smooth and creamy.

LINE × BAKE × FILL

Preheat oven to 180°C/Fan 160°C/Gas 4 and place a baking tray in the oven.

Take the pastry out of the fridge and roll out on a lightly floured surface to the thickness of a £1 coin. Lift the pastry into the tart tin and press it into the corners.

Trim the excess pastry, making sure you leave a 1cm overhang, then line with baking paper and fill with baking beans. Place on the hot baking tray in the oven and bake for 18 minutes.

Remove from the oven, discard the paper and baking beans and return to the oven for another 5–7 minutes.

Remove from the oven and leave to cool for 10–15 minutes, then use a small knife to trim the edges of the pastry.

"MUNCH THOSE QUALITY OFF-CUTS."

Spoon the jam on to the base of the tart and spread it right to the edges. Scatter the peanuts over the top then pour in the filling, smoothing to the edges.

Bake for 45–50 minutes, until a skewer inserted into the centre comes out clean.

Remove from the oven and leave to cool in the tin for 20 minutes, then carefully take the tart out of the tin and place it on a wire rack to cool completely.

DÉCOR

Mix the icing sugar and jam until smooth and spoon on top of the tart.

Finally, sprinkle with the chopped peanuts.

TREAT YOUR PASTRY LIKE A BABY – BE GENTLE.

I MEAN, IT'S SOIL, INNIT? FOOTBALL PITCHES ARE NEVER PERFECT … WELL, AT THE END OF THE GAME THEY AREN'T!

COME ON YOU REDS

There's no hiding the fact that I'm a massive Manchester United supporter. This cake is inspired by the best football team in the world but, hey, if you don't agree with me, change the colour of the cake. I won't be angry ... promise!

SERVES 16-24

Chocolate Sponge

415g caster sugar

400g plain flour

70g cocoa powder

½ tsp fine sea salt

1½ tsp bicarbonate of soda

150g dark chocolate chips

260ml cold instant coffee

260ml buttermilk

240ml vegetable oil

4 large eggs

Red Velvet Sponge

250g unsalted butter, softened

600g caster sugar

4 large eggs

40g cocoa powder

80ml red food colouring

2 tsp vanilla extract

600g plain flour

2 tsp fine sea salt

500ml buttermilk

2 tbsp apple cider vinegar

2 tsp bicarbonate of soda

Vanilla Buttercream

900g unsalted butter, softened

1.95kg icing sugar

150–180ml whole milk

2 tsp vanilla extract

yellow, red and green food gel

6 Oreos, crushed to a crumb

You will need 4 × 25cm cake tins

Preheat oven to 180°C/Fan 160°C/Gas 4 and grease and line the cake tins.

CHOCOLATE CHIP SPONGE

Sift your sugar, flour, cocoa powder, salt and bicarbonate of soda into a large bowl. Add your chocolate chips.

Combine your coffee, buttermilk, vegetable oil and eggs in a separate bowl and give it a light whisk.

Add the dry ingredients to the wet ingredients in 3 batches, mixing thoroughly after each addition.

Divide your mixture evenly between two of the cake tins and bake for 25–30 minutes, or until the sponges bounce back slightly when you press them gently.

Remove from the oven and allow to cool for 10–15 minutes in the tins before turning out on to a wire rack.

Increase the oven temperature to 190°C/Fan 170°C/Gas 5.

BRING ON THE RED

Cream your butter and sugar together in a large bowl with a free-standing or hand-held mixer until light and fluffy.

Crack the eggs in one at a time, mixing after each addition.

Once all the eggs are incorporated, scrape down the sides of the bowl to make sure that it is all thoroughly mixed, then give it one more blast.

Meanwhile, measure the cocoa powder, food colouring and vanilla into a small bowl and mix to form a paste.

Add to the cake mixture and beat until well combined and bright red.

Sift your flour and salt into a separate bowl, then add a third to the cake mixture. Mix well then add half your buttermilk. Add more flour, mix again, then add the remaining buttermilk and finish with the last of the flour.

Finally, mix the vinegar and bicarbonate of soda together in a small bowl and stir it into the cake mixture by hand so you don't overmix the batter.

Divide the mixture evenly between the remaining two cake tins and bake for 20–25 minutes.

Remove from the oven and allow to cool for 10–15 minutes in the tins before turning out on to a wire rack.

TURN OVER ⟹

CRACK ON WITH YOUR BUTTERCREAM

Measure your butter into a large bowl and beat with your free-standing or hand-held mixer until light and pale.

Sift your icing sugar into a separate bowl, then add it to the butter in 3 stages, beating after each addition. Scrape down the sides of the bowl from time to time.

Add your milk to loosen the buttercream and give it one more mix.

Separate the buttercream into 3 bowls.

Colour one bowl a bright golden yellow by dipping toothpicks into your yellow food gel, then swirling it in the buttercream to achieve the right colour. You are going to use this buttercream to crumb coat the cake.

CAKE ... ASSEMBLE!!

Use a cake leveller or sharp knife to trim the top off all the cakes so they are level.

Spread a small amount of white buttercream on a board that is slightly bigger than your sponges and place your first chocolate chip sponge on top. Place that board on a turntable, if you have one.

Spread a good dollop of white buttercream on the first layer of sponge then place a red velvet sponge on top. Now use the yellow buttercream to cover the top of this sponge. Top with the second chocolate chip sponge and cover the top of this with white buttercream. Sandwich the last red velvet sponge on top, making sure it is placed upside down on top.

CRUMB COAT * COLOUR COAT

Using a palette knife, cake scraper and a turntable, coat the sides and top of the cake with a thin layer of yellow buttercream.

Place in the fridge for at least an hour to set.

Split one bowl of white buttercream evenly between two bowls and colour one red and the other green for the grass.

Place both buttercreams into individual piping bags and snip off the ends. Alternating the red and yellow buttercream, pipe another layer around the sides of the cake. Spread the green buttercream on top with a palette knife. Smooth out the sides of the cake with a cake scraper or pallet knife – you are aiming for a cool ombre effect. Rough up the green buttercream to make a patch of grass on top.

DÉCOR

Place the remaining white buttercream in another piping bag with a narrow nozzle and draw the lines of the football pitch. Go with the goals on either side and a half-way line.

Finally, sprinkle the crushed Oreos around the base your cake.

THE BROWNIE

I think there should be a law that every single recipe book – actually every book – should have a brownie recipe. If you like 'em fudgy, dense fudgy, check it … Okay, it's fair to say this brownie recipe makes a pretty hefty brownie because, trust me, we've all been there when we say we wish there was more, but there isn't. I've got this. Once the mixture is made, don't be afraid to add to it – cookie pieces, salted caramel, candied bacon, pretzels – ahhh, damn, that's a recipe in itself … But, you know what I mean. Enjoy guys!

MAKES ABOUT 15 PIECES

300g dark chocolate (70% cocoa solids), broken into chunks

225g unsalted butter, cubed

190g dark muscovado sugar

190g golden caster sugar

½ tsp vanilla extract

6 large eggs

130g plain flour

½ tsp fine sea salt

3 tbsp cocoa powder, plus extra for dusting

You will need a 20 × 30cm baking tin

Preheat oven to 180°C/Fan 160°C/Gas 4 and grease the baking tin and line with baking paper.

MELT YOUR CHOCOLATE

Melt your chocolate in a heatproof bowl over a bain-marie (see page 205) or in the microwave, heating in 20-second bursts.

Remove the bowl from the pan and the residual heat will continue the melting process.

Whisk in both sugars and the vanilla.

Crack in the eggs one at a time and keep whisking. The mixture should be slightly bubbling.

GET YOUR DRY SERVES

Sift your dry ingredients into a separate bowl, then fold into the chocolate mixture in 3 batches, using the biggest metal spoon you have … Well, make sure it's small enough to fit in your bowl! Be gentle, though, and mix until thoroughly incorporated.

BAKE IT

Gently pour the mixture into your tin and bake for 35–40 minutes.

Remove from the oven when there is still a cheeky little wobble. The heat of the tin will continue to cook the brownie while it cools.

Leave to cool in the tin, then cut it up into unequal pieces.

For that extra finesse, sift a little cocoa powder over the top before serving.

TURN OVER ⟶

ONE TIP: YOU DON'T HAVE TO DO THIS BUT SOMETIMES I LEAVE THE BROWNIE IN THE TIN OVERNIGHT. IT'S THEN EASIER TO CUT, AND YOU KNOW WHEN PEOPLE SAY THINGS TASTE BETTER THE NEXT DAY? THIS IS ONE OF THOSE MOMENTS.

CHEEKY.

TOFFEE APPLE CRUMBLE LAYER CAKE

It is pretty evident I am obsessed with apple crumble. This cake has four layers of light brown sugar sponges, apple compote filling, and squiggles of salted caramel. And a few clusters of crumble, you know, for texture, as they say.

SERVES 16–24

Sponge

750g unsalted butter, softened
600g golden caster sugar
150g light muscovado sugar
12 large eggs
750g self-raising flour
¾ tsp baking powder
180ml whole milk
½ tsp vanilla extract

Crumble

225g plain flour
135g soft brown sugar
1 tsp fine sea salt
150g unsalted butter, cold, cubed

Cinnamon Buttercream

900g unsalted butter, softened
1.95kg icing sugar
2 tsp ground cinnamon
180ml whole milk
1½ tsp vanilla extract

Filling and Topping

1 quantity of Apple Compote (see page 117)
½ quantity of The Salted Caramel (see page 198) or 350ml shop-bought salted caramel
apple crisps (optional)

You will need 4 × 25cm cake tins

Preheat oven to 180°C/Fan 160°C/Gas 4 and grease and line the cake tins.

MAKE THOSE CAKES

Cream your butter and both sugars together in a large bowl with a free-standing or hand-held mixer until light and fluffy.

Crack the eggs in one at a time, mixing after each addition. If the mixture begins to curdle, just pop in a couple of tablespoons of the flour to bring it back together.

Turn the speed down very low and add your flour and baking powder.

Finally, add the milk and vanilla and give it one more blast.

Divide your mixture evenly between the cake tins and bake for 25–30 minutes, or until a skewer inserted into the middle comes out clean.

Remove from the oven and allow to cool for 10–15 minutes in the tins before turning out on to a wire rack.

CRUMBLE TIME

Line a baking tray with baking paper.

Tip your flour, sugar and salt into a large bowl and give it a good mix. Take the cubes of butter and begin to rub them into the flour. Keep rubbing – remember you want clustery crumble.

Tip the crumble on to the baking tray and bake for 25–30 minutes, until deep golden brown. Remove from the oven and leave to cool.

Now take this opportunity to relieve some stress – SMASH IT! Tip into an airtight container ready for later.

BUTTERCREAM

Measure your butter into a large bowl and beat with your free-standing or hand-held mixer until light and pale.

Sift your icing sugar and cinnamon into a separate bowl, then add it to the butter in 3 stages, beating after each addition. Scrape down the sides of the bowl from time to time.

Add your milk and vanilla to loosen the buttercream and give it one more mix.

ASSEMBLE

Use a cake leveller or sharp knife to trim the top off all the cakes so they are level.

Spread a small amount of buttercream on a board that is slightly bigger than your sponges and place your first layer of sponge on top. Place that board on a turntable, if you have one.

Place half the buttercream in a piping bag, snip the end and pipe a circle around the edge of the first layer of sponge, leaving a 10cm circle in the middle. Fill that circle with apple compote and sprinkle with crumble. Spoon the caramel into a piping bag and cut the tip off, then squiggle the salted caramel on top. Repeat until all the sponges are stacked. Your last sponge should be placed upside down on top.

CRUMB COAT

Using a palette knife, cake scraper and a turntable, coat the outside and top of the cake with a thin layer of the remaining buttercream.

Place in the fridge for at least an hour to set.

FINALE

Remove the cake from the fridge and apply another layer of buttercream around the sides and top of the cake.

Use any leftover buttercream to pipe around the top edges of your cake.

Finally, place apple crisps on top with more crumble and – YES – MORE SALTED CARAMEL!

THE CHEESECAKE THAT IS BAKED WELL

All right, let's get one thing straight – anything, absolutely anything, Bakewell flavoured and I'm there, before anyone, before anything. Hey, I'm there before it's even been made. And if it's in the form of a cheesecake … Well, man, what else is there to say?

SERVES 12

Biscuit Base

200g shortbread biscuits
100g flaked almonds, toasted
100g unsalted butter, melted

Filling

900g full-fat cream cheese
200ml soured cream
200g golden caster sugar
4 tbsp plain flour
¼ tsp vanilla extract
¾ tsp almond extract
3 large eggs
200g cherry jam
25g flaked almonds, toasted

Décor

200g double cream
2 tbsp golden caster sugar
¼ tsp almond extract
100g cherry jam
6–8 maraschino cherries (optional)
25g flaked almonds, toasted

You will need a 23cm springform tin

Preheat oven to 200°C/Fan 180°C/Gas 6 and line the base and sides of the tin with baking paper.

BISCUIT BASE

Double-bag the biscuits and almonds and crush them with a rolling pin or whizz them in a food-processor – either way, smash them to crumbs.

Tip the crumbs into a large bowl and stir in the butter.

Press into the base of the tin and bake for 12 minutes.

Remove from the oven and set aside.

CRACK ON WITH THE FILLING

Beat the cream cheese in a large bowl with a hand-held or free-standing mixer until creamy.

Tip in your soured cream and sugar and give it another mix to combine.

Add the flour and vanilla and almond extracts and mix again.

Finally, crack the eggs in one at a time. Mix slowly now to incorporate the eggs, you don't want the cheesecake to crack on the surface when it is baked.

Pour half the filling on top of the biscuit base. Dot with a couple of tablespoons of the cherry jam and give it a swirl with a knife to create a marble effect.

Top with the remaining cheesecake filling and finish with the remaining cherry jam dollops. Smooth the top.

BAKE IT

Place in the middle of the oven and bake for 12 minutes.

Remove from the oven, sprinkle with the almond flakes and drop the oven temperature to 150°C/Fan 130°C/Gas 2. Return to the oven and bake for another 35–40 minutes.

> "THE CHEESECAKE SHOULD HAVE A CHEEKY WOBBLE IN THE MIDDLE."

Switch off the oven and leave the cheesecake inside with the door closed for 1 hour.

Now, open the oven door and leave the cheesecake inside with the door slightly ajar for another hour.

YEH, I KNOW, ANOTHER HOUR ...

Remove from the oven and leave to cool at room temperature for a third hour.

Cover with clingfilm and leave in the fridge overnight.

THE BAKEWELL DOLLOP

Carefully remove the cheesecake from the tin and peel off the baking paper. Place it on a large serving plate.

Whisk the double cream, sugar and almond extract in a medium bowl to soft peaks.

Fold in the cherry jam to give a ripple effect.

Place the cherry cream into a piping bag with a star-tipped nozzle and pipe rosettes around the edge of your cake. Put a cherry on top of each rosette, if you like, and finish off with a sprinkle of almonds.

PLANTAIN TARTE TATIN

This is my take on a classic apple tarte tatin. Instead of using apples, though, let's use some plantain and add a rummy, spicy dollop of whipped cream.

SERVES 6

Tarte Tatin

100g golden caster sugar

85g unsalted butter

5 firm plantains, slice into 2cm-thick circles

generous pinch of fine sea salt

zest of 1 orange

1 × 500g pack ready-rolled puff pastry

Whipped Spicy Dollop

300ml double cream

3 tbsp icing sugar

4 tbsp dark rum

½ tsp ground ginger

zest of 1 orange

¼ tsp cayenne pepper

1½ tsp ground cinnamon

1 tsp ground cloves

100g raisins

You will need a 23cm cake tin with a solid base

Preheat oven to 200°C/Fan 180°C/Gas 6.

SORT THAT CARAMEL

Place the sugar and butter in a heavy-based saucepan over a low heat. Do not stir the mixture.

As soon as the sugar has melted, crank up the heat and allow it to bubble. You are looking for a super-deep caramel colour.

Pour into the cake tin and quickly spread it out evenly. Use a warm spoon because you don't want the caramel to harden.

Arrange the plantain slices in a circular pattern over the caramel, then sprinkle over the salt and orange zest.

PASTRY × BAKE

Cut the pastry into a 26cm circle (it needs to be larger than the tin), then lay it on top of the plantain and tuck the edges down inside the tin.

Bake for 30 minutes, until the pastry has risen and is golden and cooked through.

Allow the tart to cool in the tin for 1–2 minutes then – this is the scary part, nah, not really – carefully turn it out on to a large serving plate.

WHIP IT UP

Meanwhile, whisk the double cream with the icing sugar in a medium bowl until soft peaks are formed.

Add the rum, ginger, orange zest, cayenne pepper, cinnamon, cloves and raisins and continue to whisk until just combined.

Serve each slice of tart with a massive dollop of the spiced cream.

IF YOU'VE GOT RHUBARB AND CUSTARD SWEETS, YOU KNOW THE DEAL – SMASH 'EM AND SPRINKLE.

RHUBARB ✕ CUSTARD

I had a slight obsession with those cool, old-school sweet shops.
One sweet that always stuck out for me was the half 'n' half rhubarb and custard.

SERVES 16-24

Sponge
500g unsalted butter, softened
500g golden caster sugar
8 large eggs
½ tsp vanilla extract
½ tsp almond extract
350g self-raising flour
170g ground almonds
1 tsp baking powder
zest of 1 orange
200ml whole milk

Ginger Crème Pat
500ml whole milk
1 tbsp vanilla extract
1 tsp ground ginger
125g golden caster sugar
6 large egg yolks
80g plain flour
200ml double cream
75g stem ginger, diced

Rhubarb Filling
1 tbsp cornflour
2 tbsp water
500g rhubarb
zest and juice of 1 large orange
75g caster sugar

Vanilla Buttercream
600g unsalted butter, softened
1.3kg icing sugar
150–180ml whole milk
1 tsp vanilla extract

To Finish
pink food colouring
yellow food colouring
Rhubarb and custard sweets,
crushed (optional)

You will need 4 × 20cm cake tins

Preheat oven to 160°C/Fan 140°C/Gas 3 and grease and line the cake tins.

SPONGE TIME

Cream your butter and sugar together in a large bowl with a free-standing or hand-held mixer until light and fluffy.

Crack the eggs in one at a time, mixing after each addition. If the mixture begins to curdle, just pop in a couple of tablespoons of the flour to bring it back together.

Turn the speed down low and add both your extracts, flour, ground almonds, baking powder, orange zest and milk.

Divide your mixture evenly between the cake tins and bake for 30 minutes, or until a skewer inserted into the middle comes out clean.

Remove from the oven and allow to cool for 10–15 minutes in the tins before turning out on to a wire rack.

CRÈME PAT

Place a saucepan over a medium heat and add the milk, vanilla and ginger. Bring to the boil then take off the heat.

Meanwhile, whisk the sugar and egg yolks together in a large bowl. Sift your flour into the bowl and mix together.

Pour a little of the milk into the sugar mixture, constantly whisking, then whisk in the remaining hot milk, pouring it in a steady stream until it is well combined.

Pour the custard back into the saucepan and place over a gentle heat. Keep stirring until thick.

Remove from the heat and pass the custard through a sieve. Place a sheet of clingfilm over the surface of the custard to prevent a skin from forming. Leave to cool then pop in the fridge.

Meanwhile, whip the cream in a large bowl until thick. Fold the cream into your chilled custard then add your stem ginger. Pop back in the fridge until you're ready to use.

RHUBARB FILLING

Mix the cornflour and water together in a small bowl with a fork.

Chop the rhubarb into medium-sized pieces and place in a large saucepan with the orange zest and juice, sugar, cornflour mixture and another tablespoon of water.

Place over a medium heat and bring to the boil. Turn down the heat and simmer for 5–7 minutes, or until the rhubarb is cooked but not soggy – it needs to hold its shape.

Remove from the heat and tip into a bowl to cool.

TURN OVER ⟶

BUTTERCREAM TIME

Measure your butter into a large bowl and beat with your free-standing or hand-held mixer until light and pale.

Sift your icing sugar into a separate bowl, then add it to the butter in 3 stages, beating after each addition. Scrape down the sides of the bowl from time to time.

Add your milk and vanilla to loosen the buttercream and then beat it again until it holds its shape.

ASSEMBLE

Use a cake leveller or sharp knife to trim the top off all the cakes so they are level.

Spread a small amount of buttercream on a board that is slightly bigger than your sponges and place your first layer of sponge on top. Place that board on a turntable, if you have one.

Place half the buttercream in a piping bag with a round-tipped nozzle and pipe a circle around the edge of the first layer of sponge, leaving an 8cm circle in the middle. Fill that circle with half the stewed rhubarb.

Repeat this process with another layer of sponge, but fill the circle with the custard filling. Top with another sponge, pipe a buttercream circle and fill it with the rhubarb filling. Finally, top with the last sponge, making sure it is placed upside down on top.

CRUMB AND TOP COAT

Using a palette knife, cake scraper and a turntable, coat the sides and top of the cake with a thin layer of buttercream. Place in the fridge for at least an hour to set.

Separate the remaining buttercream into two bowls. Colour one bowl with pink food colouring and the other with yellow food colouring. Place both buttercreams into individual piping bags with round-tipped nozzles.

Alternating the pink and yellow buttercream, pipe another layer around the sides and top of the cake.

Smooth the surface with a palette knife – you should have a cool, flurry, sweet shop effect.

Pipe alternate buttercream kisses around the top edge of your cake, and scatter over the crushed sweets, if you like.

SALTED MILLIONAIRE DOMINOES

Hands down, one of my favourite bakes known to man, woman, boy, girl and pigeon – millionaire shortbread. However, I always thought it needed a couple of extra elements to make it, hmmm, how can I say it? Cheeky.

MAKES ABOUT 36

Shortbread Base

345g unsalted butter, cold, cubed

180g golden caster sugar

345g plain flour

180g rice flour

1 tsp fine sea salt

1 tsp vanilla extract

Salted Peanut Butter Caramel

180ml double cream

1 tsp vanilla extract

370g caster sugar

60g liquid glucose

300g salted butter, cubed

2 tbsp Classic Smooth (see page 199) or shop-bought smooth peanut butter

50g dry-roasted peanuts, roughly chopped

Chocolate Topping

500g dark chocolate (70% cocoa solids), broken into chunks

1 quantity of Royal icing (see page 32)

You will need 3 silicone trays with 12 8 × 3cm moulds or two 24 × 18cm baking tins and a food thermometer

The food thermometer is used for measuring the temperature of the chocolate (see page 116). This is to ensure a nice shiny finish but isn't absolutely necessary if you don't own a thermometer.

Pop a baking tray into your freezer before you start doing anything. It will make sense later. Preheat oven to 200°C/Fan 160°C/Gas 6. If using baking tins, grease and line with baking paper.

SHORTBREAD BASE

Place all your ingredients in a food-processor and whizz until it just begins to come together.

Tip on to your work surface and knead gently until it does come together.

Weigh out 25g balls of the shortbread (see page 205) and press into the silicone moulds, or divide the mixture between the baking tins.

Bake for 15 minutes, until golden. (If baking in the 2 tins they might need an extra 5 minutes.)

YOU KNOW WHAT TIME IT IS

Measure the cream and vanilla into a saucepan and place over a medium heat. Bring to the boil then remove from the heat and put to one side.

Place another saucepan over a medium heat and, when it is hot, add roughly one-third of the sugar with the liquid glucose. Heat slowly until the sugar crystals have dissolved and it forms a light caramel.

Add the remaining sugar and continue to cook until you get an amber caramel – this will take 15 minutes.

Pour the warm cream into the caramel, mix well then remove from the heat.

Add small chunks of butter, a little at a time, mixing to melt.

Stir in the peanut butter.

Place the pan back on the heat and bring the caramel up to a final temperature of 120°C using a food thermometer.

Remove your baking tray from the freezer and pour your caramel on to it and give it a good stir. This will help the cooling process.

Fold your dry-roasted peanuts into the caramel then distribute evenly over the shortbread bases.

Place your caramel shortbreads in your freezer for 10 minutes then transfer to the fridge to finish setting.

Make the royal icing as on page 32.

TURN OVER ⟶

CHOCOLATE TOPPING

Melt 330g of the dark chocolate using a bain-marie (see page 205) to a temperature of 45–50°C. Tip the remaining chocolate into the bowl and stir until 31–32°C is reached.

Spread a thin layer of chocolate over the top of all the caramel shortbreads. Leave to set.

Carefully pop out each piece of shortbread or turn the two slabs out of the baking tins and cut into 8 × 3cm slices. Then line them up.

Place the royal icing in a piping bag with a thin-tipped nozzle and pipe a domino effect on each shortbread.

ALWAYS ROOM FOR CRUMBLE

All right, I know I've said it already but I'm obsessed with anything to do with apple crumble, but it has to be served with custard. You might think that crumble is a winter dessert but I've put this classic pudding in a pastry case to serve as a tart on even the hottest days.

SERVES 12

Crème Pat

750ml whole milk

1 tsp vanilla extract

a grating of nutmeg

150g caster sugar

6 large egg yolks

60g cornflour

60g unsalted butter

Apple Compote

2 Bramley apples, peeled, cored and diced

3 Granny Smith apples, peeled, cored and diced

2 Pink Lady apples, peeled, cored and diced

juice of 1 lemon

50g unsalted butter

100g caster sugar

2 tsp ground cinnamon

2 tbsp cornflour

4 tbsp water

Crumble Topping

350g plain flour

170g muscovado sugar

200g unsalted butter, cold, cubed

Pastry

400g plain flour, plus extra for dusting

250g unsalted butter, cold, cubed

2 tbsp caster sugar

1 large egg

2 tbsp cold water

1 large egg yolk, beaten

You'll need 12 × 10cm tart tins

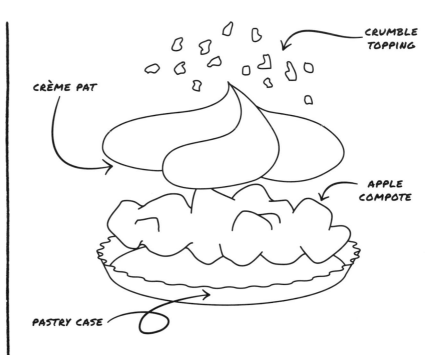

CRUMBLE TOPPING

CRÈME PAT

APPLE COMPOTE

PASTRY CASE

CRÈME PAT A DAY AHEAD

Place a saucepan over a medium heat and add the milk, vanilla and nutmeg. Bring to the boil then take off the heat.

Meanwhile, whisk the sugar, egg yolks and cornflour together in a large bowl.

Pour a little of the milk into the sugar mixture, constantly whisking, then whisk in the remaining hot milk, pouring it in a steady stream until it is well combined.

Pour the custard back into the saucepan and place over a fairly gentle heat – you don't want scrambled eggs. Keep stirring until thick. It will just come to the boil.

Remove from the heat and pass the custard through a sieve. Add the butter and stir until melted.

Pop a sheet of clingfilm on the surface of the custard to stop a skin from forming and set aside. Once cool, place in the fridge to chill overnight.

TURN OVER ⟹

COMPOTE A DAY AHEAD

Place all the apples in a large saucepan with the lemon juice, butter, sugar and cinnamon.

Mix the cornflour and water together with a fork in a small bowl then pour this over the apples. Give the apples a stir, then place the pan over a low-medium heat and cook gently, stirring occasionally.

This is probably the best part – taste the compote every now and then, because it depends on how mushy you want your apples to be. Let's see if you've got the apple "tekkers" – you want some of the chunks to be completely cooked through but some to keep their bite. Trust me, it's the best of both worlds.

Once your desired consistency is achieved, pop the apple compote into a bowl and set aside.

Once cool, place in the fridge ready for tomorrow.

CRUMBLE A DAY AHEAD

Preheat oven to 180°C/Fan 160°C/Gas 4 and line a baking tray with baking paper.

Tip your flour and sugar into a large bowl and give it a good mix.

Rub the butter into the flour – you want clustery clusters of crumble.

Place the crumble on the baking tray and cook for 25–30 minutes, until a deep golden brown.

Remove from the oven and leave to one side to cool.

Then – erm, how can I say this in the nicest way possible? – SMASH IT! Crumble the crumble because this is going to be sprinkled on top of your tarts. Tip into an airtight container ready for tomorrow.

PASTRY ON BAKING DAY

Tip the flour, butter and sugar into a food-processor and pulse until it resembles fine breadcrumbs.

Crack the egg into a bowl and beat lightly with the cold water.

While the motor is running, add the egg and water mixture and pulse until it starts to come together. Do not let the dough whizz round or it will become overworked.

Tip the pastry on to a lightly floured work surface and gently bring it together. Wrap in clingfilm and stick in the fridge for at least an hour to chill.

TIME TO BAKE

Preheat oven to 200°C/Fan 180°C/Gas 6 and place two baking trays in the oven to heat up.

Remove the pastry from the fridge and lightly flour your work surface. Roll out the pastry to a thickness of a £1 coin, cut out 10cm circles and use to fill the tart tins. Return to the fridge to rest for a further 15 minutes.

Place squares of baking paper over the pastry in each pie tin and fill with baking beans. Carefully place your tart tins on the hot baking trays in the oven and bake for 15–17 minutes.

Remove the baking beans and paper from the tins, then brush with the beaten egg yolk. Return to the oven for a further 7 minutes.

Remove from the oven and leave to cool for a few minutes before giving your tart cases a "fresh trim" and lifting out on to a wire rack to finish cooling.

PIE TIME

Spread a generous amount of apple compote on to the base of each pie.

Place your crème pat in a piping bag with a round-tipped nozzle and, using a circular motion going inwards, pipe the custard over the top of the apple filling.

Finish with a good sprinkling of the crumble and WHAM ... FINISHED!

"IF YOU HAPPEN TO STUMBLE ACROSS A TUB OF ICE CREAM IN THE FREEZER, OR YOU'VE MADE MY ICE CREAM FROM PAGE 186 (WINK, WINK), IT'LL BE THE DESSERT OF ALL DESSERTS."

STICKY TOFFEE TOWER

Usually this is either one massive pudding plonked in the middle of the table, or a few mini ones that seem a little lost. How about 14 decent-sized puddings stacked on top of each other, topped with banana and toasted pecans, slathered in a sea of caramel sauce? I call this theatre in food.

SERVES 14

Puddings

450g Medjool dates, stoned and chopped into small pieces

350ml boiling water

2 tsp vanilla extract

170g unsalted butter, softened

140g demerara sugar

140g light soft brown sugar

4 large eggs, beaten

2 tbsp black treacle

2 tbsp golden syrup

350g self-raising flour

2 tsp bicarbonate of soda

200ml whole milk

3 bananas, cut into ½cm-thick circles, plus extra for decoration

For the Sauce

250ml The Salted Caramel (see page 198) or shop-bought salted caramel

2–3 tbsp dark rum (optional)

200g pecans, toasted

You will need 14 × 250ml pudding tins

Pop the dates in a large bowl and pour the boiling water over them. Leave to sit for 30 minutes. You want them cool and well soaked.

Mash the dates with a fork then add your vanilla extract.

> "IF YOU REALLY DON'T WANT TO FEEL SMALL CHUNKS OF DATES IN THE PUDDINGS, THOUGH, YOU CAN BLITZ THEM TO A PULP IN A FOOD-PROCESSER."

Preheat oven to 180°C/Fan 160°C/Gas 4 and grease and flour the mini pudding tins and line with baking paper. Do this properly — trust me, it's worth it. You want all the puddings to come out of the tins!

> "LET'S BE HONEST, WHO HAS 14 PUDDING TINS IN THEIR HOUSE? IF YOU DON'T, JUST BAKE THEM IN BATCHES. IT WILL TAKE SLIGHTLY LONGER BUT IT'LL BE WORTH THE WAIT."

CRACK ON WITH YOUR PUDDINGS

Cream the butter and both sugars together in a large bowl with a free-standing or hand-held mixer until creamy. It won't be that smooth as the demerara is grainy but it's a great sugar to use.

Add the eggs a little at a time, mixing well after each addition.

Beat in the treacle and golden syrup.

Sift your flour and bicarbonate of soda into a separate bowl then gently fold some into the butter mixture, using a large spoon.

Gently stir in half your milk then fold in more flour. Repeat this process until everything is well combined.

Finally, stir in the soaked dates.

TURN OVER ⟹

BAKE THEM

Place a few circles of banana into the base of each pudding tin.

Divide the mixture evenly between the pudding tins, then pop the tins on to some baking trays and bake for 20–25 minutes, or until well risen.

Remove from the oven and leave to cool in their tins on a wire rack.

RUM CARAMEL

Make the salted caramel as page 198 and add the rum with the double cream. Stir and leave to bubble for a couple of minutes. Continue to make the caramel as usual.

If you use shop-bought caramel, warm it in a saucepan over a medium heat then stir in the rum. Leave to bubble for a few minutes before using.

IT'S TIME

To take the puddings out of the moulds, turn them upside down and give the base a gentle tap. They should just pop out. If they don't, get a knife or off-set palette knife and gently run it around the edges of the puddings, give the base another tap and it should do the trick. If it doesn't then ... run!

"SERIOUSLY, THOUGH, DON'T WORRY ABOUT IT. SCOOP OUT AS MUCH AS YOU CAN WITH A SPOON AND IF YOU LOSE SOME IN THE PROCESS, GET CREATIVE. HAVE SOME OF THE PUDDINGS LEANING, TOPSY TURVY, THE LOT."

Create a pyramid with the puddings, 9 for the base, 4 in the middle then 1 on top – square numbers, innit.

Pour the caramel sauce from the top, it should drip all the way down to the base.

Finish off with a good sprinkle of toasted pecans and some extra slices of banana.

CHILLED RICE PUDDING CRÈME BRÛLÉE

Okay, okay, I get it. Rice pudding is one of those things that you want to love but looking at it can be a little upsetting. It all tastes the same and, let's be honest, it's boring to look at. But, here's the question – if you were going to serve it as a dessert, how would you level up the humble school dinner into a cheeky treat? I know, how about . . .

SERVES 6

Blackberry and Pear Compote

5 ripe pears, peeled and cored

200g blackberries, frozen or fresh

1 tsp vanilla extract

knob of butter

¼ tsp fine sea salt

zest of 1 lemon

**White Chocolate ×
Cardamom Rice Pudding**

100g pudding rice

550ml whole milk

250ml double cream

1 tsp vanilla extract

90g sugar

½ tsp ground cardamom

150g white chocolate (30% cocoa solids), broken into chunks

To Finish

caster sugar, to cover

You will need 6 × 10cm ramekins and a blowtorch

BLACKBERRY AND PEAR COMPOTE

Place the pears in a large pot over a medium heat and add the blackberries, vanilla, butter, salt and lemon zest. Slowly bring to the boil, then reduce the heat and simmer for 10–12 minutes, until thick and glossy with the blackberries holding their shape.

PUDDING TIME

Measure the rice, milk, cream, vanilla, sugar and cardamom into a large, heavy-based saucepan and place over a medium heat. Bring to the boil, stirring continuously.

Reduce the heat and simmer gently for about 50 minutes, until the rice has plumped up and the liquid has reduced.

Keep on stirring and, when the rice is tender, remove from the heat add the white chocolate, then stir until fully melted.

Pop a sheet of clingfilm on the surface of the rice and leave to cool to room temperature.

Transfer to the fridge until cold.

SERVE IT UP

Divide the blackberry and pear compote evenly between 6 ramekins, then top with the chilled rice pudding.

Finally, give all ramekins a generous sprinkling of caster sugar then hit them with the blowtorch to get your brulée. If you don't have a blowtorch then it's fine to put under a hot grill for a couple of minutes to melt the sugar. You won't get the amazing crunch but it will do the job.

AY, DON'T FORGET TO STIR THE RICE SO IT DOESN'T STICK TO THE PAN.

TURN OVER ⟹

SALTED NUTTER

I don't wanna say too much, but this is basically me in cake form.

SERVES 16-24

Peanut Butter Sponge

250g unsalted butter, softened

100g Classic Smooth (see page 199) or shop-bought smooth peanut butter

250g caster sugar

4 large eggs

150g self-raising flour

½ tsp baking powder

60ml whole milk

½ tsp vanilla extract

Vanilla Sponge

250g unsalted butter, softened

125g golden caster sugar

125g dark muscovado sugar

4 large eggs

250g self-raising flour

½ tsp baking powder

60ml whole milk

½ tsp vanilla extract

Salted Caramel Buttercream

450g unsalted butter, softened

975g icing sugar

90ml whole milk

4 tbsp The Salted Caramel (see page 198) or shop-bought salted caramel

1 tsp vanilla extract

Chocolate Buttercream

140g unsalted butter, softened

215g icing sugar

60g cocoa powder

75ml whole milk

Peanut Butter Buttercream

150g unsalted butter, softened

60g peanut butter

325g icing sugar

45ml whole milk

Preheat oven to 180°C/Fan 160°C/Gas 4 and grease and line the cake tins.

PEANUT BUTTER SPONGE

Cream your butter, peanut butter and sugar in a large bowl, using a hand-held or free-standing mixer, until light and fluffy.

Crack in the eggs one at a time, beating after each addition, until well incorporated.

Turn the speed down very low and add your flour and baking powder.

Add the milk and vanilla to loosen the mixture, and continue to mix on low speed. You may want to scrape down the sides of the bowl just to make sure everything is mixed in.

Divide the mixture evenly between two of the tins and bake for 20–25 minutes, until a skewer poked in the middle comes out clean.

Remove the cakes from the oven and leave them to cool in their tins for about 10–15 minutes, then turn out on to a wire rack to finish cooling.

VANILLA SPONGE

Cream your butter and both sugars in a large bowl, using a hand-held or free-standing mixer, until light and fluffy.

Crack in the eggs, one at a time, beating after each addition, until well incorporated.

Turn the speed down very low and add your flour and baking powder.

Add the milk and vanilla to loosen the mixture, and continue to mix on low speed. You may want to scrape down the sides of the bowl just to make sure everything is mixed in.

Divide the mixture evenly between the two remaining tins and bake for 20–25 minutes, until a skewer poked in the middle comes out clean.

Remove the cakes from the oven and leave them to cool in their tins for about 10–15 minutes, then turn out on to a wire rack to finish cooling.

SALTED CARAMEL BUTTERCREAM

Beat your butter in a large bowl with your hand-held or free-standing mixer, until light and pale.

Sift your icing sugar into a separate bowl, then add it to the butter mixture in 3 stages, beating after each addition. Scrape down the sides of the bowl from time to time.

Add your milk, salted caramel and vanilla to loosen the buttercream and beat again.

TURN OVER FOR MORE INGREDIENTS

Décor and Filling

¼ quantity of The Brownie (see page 101) or 200g shop-bought brownies, chopped into 1cm squares

6 × Would You Risk It For A . . . cookies (see page 171) or shop-bought chocolate chip cookies, half crumbled

cocoa powder, to sprinkle

3–5 giant pretzels

You will need 4 × 20cm cake tins

ASSEMBLE

Use a cake leveller or sharp knife to trim the top off all the cakes so they are level.

Spread a small amount of buttercream on a board that is slightly bigger than your sponges and place your first peanut butter sponge on top. Place that board on a turntable, if you have one.

Spread a thin layer of buttercream on the sponge and stick a couple of pieces of brownie and cookie on top. Top with a vanilla sponge, then repeat the buttercream. Continue to stack, alternating the sponges and sticking brownies and cookies in between each layer, making sure your last sponge is placed upside down on the top.

Using a palette knife, cake scraper and a turntable, coat the sides and top of the cake with a thin layer of buttercream until it's covered.

Place your cake in the fridge for at least 30 minutes to set.

Spoon any leftover salted caramel buttercream into a piping bag.

CHOCOLATE BUTTERCREAM

Beat your butter in a large bowl with your hand-held or free-standing mixer until light and pale.

Sift your icing sugar and cocoa powder into a separate bowl, then add it to the butter mixture in 3 stages, beating after each addition. Scrape down the sides of the bowl from time to time.

Add your milk to loosen the buttercream and mix again.

PEANUT BUTTER BUTTERCREAM

Beat your butter and peanut butter in a large bowl with your hand-held or free-standing mixer, until light and pale.

Sift your icing sugar into a separate bowl, then add it to the butter mixture in 3 stages, beating after each addition. Scrape down the sides of the bowl from time to time.

Add your milk to loosen the buttercream and mix again.

Place both buttercreams into individual piping bags.

FLURRY EFFECT

Snip the ends off the piping bags and take your cake out of the fridge.

Place your cake on a turntable and pipe streaks of buttercream, alternating the different flavours, until the whole cake is covered.

Using a palette knife, smooth the sides and top for a salted nutter flurry effect.

"COOL, RIGHT?"

FINISH

Sprinkle with cocoa powder and leftover cookies, brownies and the pretzels. Place them on the cake in any way you want. CREATE ART!

BECAUSE
SOMETIMES
YOU HAVE TO
DO IT FOR
THE INSTA.

CHEQ THEM UP

I made this cake for my nephew's birthday – four tiers and he was
only 10 at the time. I mean, did he really need such a massive cake? Yes, he's my
nephew! The buttercream in this recipe makes it for me.

SERVES 16-24

Chocolate Sponge

275g caster sugar

265g plain flour

50g cocoa powder

½ tsp fine sea salt

¾ tsp bicarbonate of soda

100g dark chocolate chips

175ml cold instant coffee

90ml buttermilk

90ml soured cream

160ml vegetable oil

3 eggs

Vanilla Sponge

250g unsalted butter, softened

250g caster sugar

4 eggs

250g self-raising flour

¼ tsp baking powder

60ml whole milk

½ tsp vanilla extract

M & M Crispy Buttercream

600g unsalted butter, softened

1.3kg icing sugar

120–150ml whole milk

½ tsp vanilla extract

2 × 121g Crispy M&Ms, crushed

Ganache Drip

250ml double cream

200g dark chocolate (70% cocoa
solids), broken into chunks

**You will need 4 × 20cm cake
tins, a 12cm cutter and a 6cm
cutter**

Preheat oven to 180°C/Fan 160°C/Gas 4
and grease and line the cake tins.

CHOCOLATE SPONGE

Sift your sugar, flour, cocoa powder, salt
and bicarbonate of soda into a large
bowl. Add your chocolate chips.

Combine your coffee, buttermilk, soured
cream, vegetable oil and eggs in a
separate bowl and give it a light whisk.

Add the dry ingredients to the wet
ingredients in 3 batches, mixing
thoroughly after each addition.

Divide the mixture evenly between two
of the tins and bake for 25–30 minutes,
or until the sponges bounce back slightly
when you press them gently.

Remove from the oven and allow to
cool for 10–15 minutes in the tins before
turning out on to a wire rack.

VANILLA SPONGE

Cream your butter and sugar in a large
bowl, using a hand-held or free-standing
mixer, until light and fluffy.

Crack in the eggs one at a time,
beating after each addition, until well
incorporated. If the mixture begins to
curdle, add a couple of tablespoons
of the flour and it should bring it back
together.

Turn the speed down very low and add
your flour and baking powder.

Add the milk and vanilla to loosen the
mixture, and continue to mix on low
speed. You may want to scrape down
the sides of the bowl just to make sure
everything is mixed in.

Divide the mixture evenly between two
of the tins and bake for 25–27 minutes,
until a skewer poked into the middle
comes out clean.

Remove from the oven and allow to
cool for 10–15 minutes in the tins before
turning out on to a wire rack.

M&M BUTTERCREAM

Beat your butter in a large bowl with a
hand-held or free-standing mixer, until
light and pale.

Sift your icing sugar into a separate bowl,
then add it to the butter in 3 stages,
beating after each addition. Scrape down
the sides of the bowl from time to time.

Add your milk and vanilla to loosen the
buttercream and give it one more mix …
SORTED!

Separate your buttercream into two
bowls and tip the contents of one of the
bags of Crispy M&Ms into one bowl and
fold them into the buttercream.

TURN OVER ⟹

CHEQ THEM UP

Use a cake leveller or sharp knife to trim the top off all the cakes so they are level. Be extremely careful with the chocolate cake as it is very dense and moist.

Now use a cutter to cut a 12cm circle out of the middle of each of the cakes (see page 207). Make sure you press down firmly so you achieve a clean cut. Remove the circles and set aside.

Next cut small 6cm circles out of the larger circles.

Place the rings of cake in one another, alternating the colours.

Spread a small amount of plain buttercream on a board that is slightly bigger than your sponges and place your first layer of sponge on top. Place that board on a turntable, if you have one.

Spread a layer of M&M buttercream on the sponge and top with another sponge, making sure the outer ring alternates in colour. Continue to stack the sponges, alternating the outer rings and making sure your last sponge is placed upside down on the top.

CRUMB ✳ FINAL COAT

Using a palette knife, cake scraper and a turntable, coat the sides and top of the cake with a thin layer of M&M buttercream until it's covered.

Place your cake in the fridge for at least an hour to set.

Finally, cover the cake with plain buttercream – for a cleaner finish – and return your cake to the fridge. Place any leftover buttercream in a piping bag with a large nozzle of your choice for decorating later.

GANACHE DRIP

Pour your cream into a saucepan and place over a low heat. Bring to a gentle simmer.

Tip your chocolate into a large bowl and pour the hot cream over the top. Leave to melt for a few minutes.

Begin to stir from the centre outwards with a wooden spoon. Continue stirring until it's a glossy and smooth consistency. You don't want to leave it too long because you still want it to be pourable.

DRIBBLE TIME!

Take the cake out of the fridge and spoon most of the ganache over the top edge, encouraging the dribble down the sides of the cake. Use any leftover ganache to fill in the top of the cake.

Pipe the leftover buttercream around the top edges of your cake and scatter some of those crispy chocolate treats over the top of the cake.

BOSH!

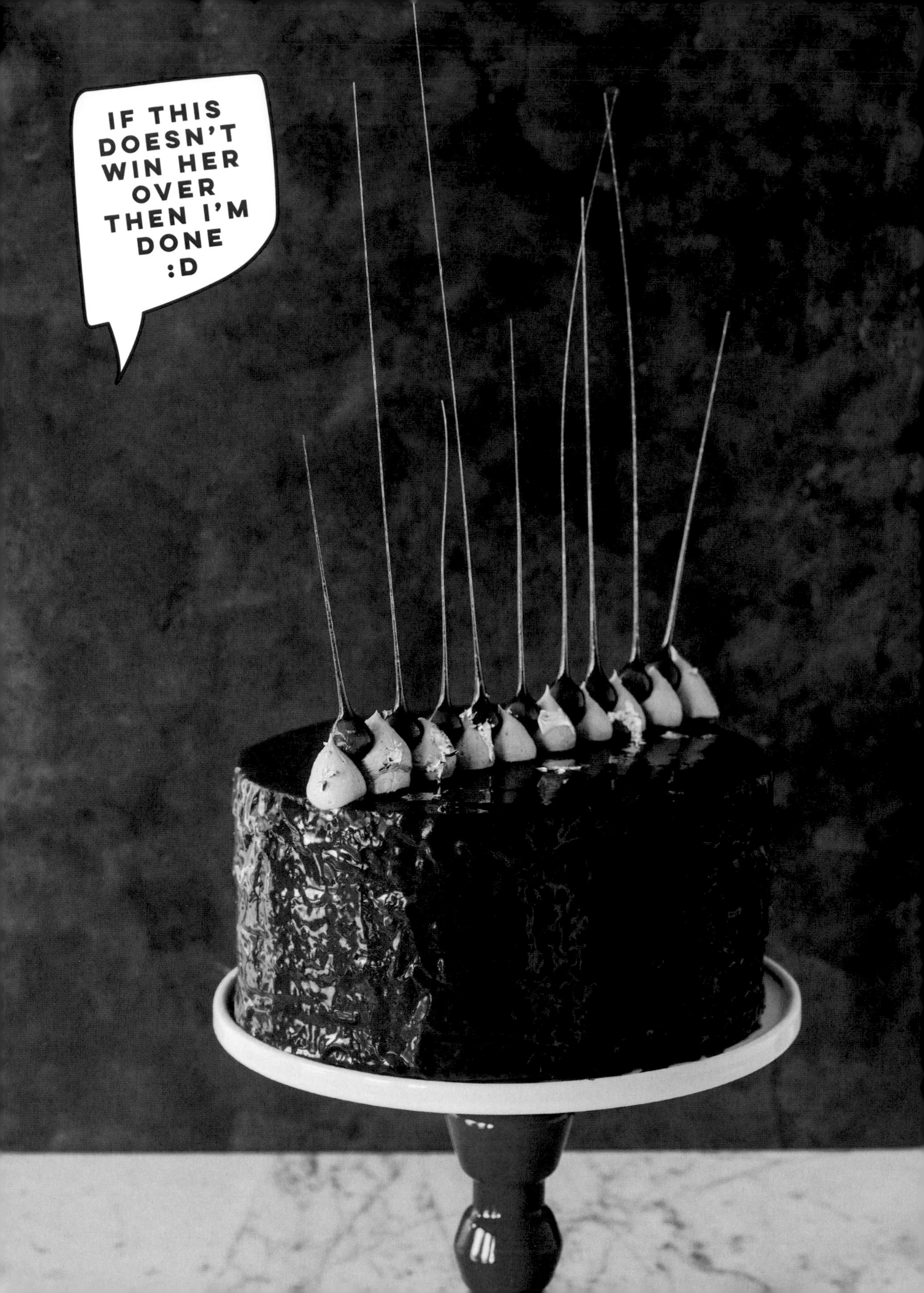
IF THIS DOESN'T WIN HER OVER THEN I'M DONE :D

OOOOO FANCY

Coffee sponge cake × chocolate hazelnut buttercream × mirror glaze × hazelnut décor: always a winner in my book. This cake was made to impress someone who I really liked in my second year of uni. I think she liked it. I just realised she could be reading this – ahh, how embarrassing!

SERVES 16-24

Coffee Sponge
60ml whole milk

250g unsalted butter, softened

125g golden caster sugar

125g light muscovado sugar

4 large eggs

250g self-raising flour

¼ tsp baking powder

2 tsp instant coffee powder

½ tsp vanilla extract

Hazelnut Swiss
4 large egg whites

300g caster sugar

400g unsalted butter, softened and cubed

100g Nutella

1 tsp vanilla extract

Ganache
200ml double cream

50g caster sugar

200g dark chocolate (70% cocoa solids), broken into chunks

Chocolate Mirror Glaze
225ml double cream

205g caster sugar

85g cocoa powder

4½ gelatine leaves

Caramelised Hazelnuts
200g granulated sugar

3–4 tbsp water

20 blanched hazelnuts

2 sheets of edible gold leaf

You will need 4 × 15cm cake tins and a food thermometer

Preheat oven to 180°C/Fan 160°C/Gas 4 and grease and line the cake tins.

COFFEE SPONGE

Place the milk in a small pan over a medium heat and stir as you bring it just to a boil. Remove from the heat and leave on the side to cool slightly.

Cream your butter and both sugars together in a large bowl with a free-standing or hand-held mixer until light and fluffy.

Crack in the eggs one at a time, beating after each addition, until well incorporated.

Turn the speed down very low and add your flour and baking powder.

Combine the warm milk with the coffee powder and add to the cake mixture with the vanilla to loosen.

Continue to mix on a low speed until everything comes together. You may want to scrape down the sides of the bowl to make sure everything is mixed in.

Divide the mixture evenly between the tins and pop in the oven for 18–20 minutes, until a skewer poked into the middle comes out clean.

Remove from the oven and cool in their tins for 10–15 minutes, then turn out on to a wire rack to finish cooling.

HAZELNUT SWISS

Prepare a bain-marie (see page 205) and place your egg whites in a heatproof bowl over the simmering water.

Tip in your sugar and whisk until it has fully dissolved. The best way to check this is to rub a bit of the mixture between your fingers – if you can't feel any sugar, it's ready.

Remove the bowl from the heat and, using your whisk attachment in your free-standing mixer or hand-held whisk on a medium to high speed, whisk for about 10 minutes, or until cool. You are aiming for super-fluffy clouds of meringue.

Now time for decadence. Add the butter in small chunks while you whisk on medium speed. Take your time with this – show your Swiss some love. The more patient you are, the nicer it will be. Before you know it, it'll look like the silky smooth Swiss we know and love.

It's pretty much done now, you just need to add two more ingredients – the Nutella and the vanilla, then give it one more whisk for luck.

TURN OVER ⟶

GANACHE FILLING

Pour your cream and sugar into a saucepan and place over a low heat. Bring to a gentle simmer.

Tip the chocolate into a large bowl and pour the hot cream over the top. Leave to melt for a few minutes then stir until a glossy and smooth consistency (see page 208).

Leave to one side to cool completely, or pop it in the fridge for 20 minutes.

Once cool, use your whisk attachment in your free-standing mixer or a hand-held whisk on a medium to high speed, to beat until light brown.

STACK 'EM

Use a cake leveller or sharp knife to trim the top off all the cakes so they are level.

Spread a small amount of hazelnut Swiss buttercream on a board that is slightly bigger than your sponges and place your first layer of sponge on top. Place that board on a turntable, if you have one.

Place the remaining buttercream in a piping bag with a round-tipped nozzle. Pipe a buttercream border on this first layer of sponge leaving an 8cm circle in the middle. Fill that circle with the chocolate ganache.

Repeat this process until all the cakes are stacked, making sure your last sponge is placed upside down on top.

Using a palette knife, cake scraper and a turntable, coat the sides and top of the cake with a thin layer of buttercream until it's covered.

Place your cake in the fridge for at least an hour to set.

Apply a final layer of buttercream around and on top of the cake and place it back into the fridge.

CHOCOLATE MIRROR GLAZE

Measure the double cream, sugar, cocoa powder and 225ml of water into a saucepan and heat gently, stirring all the time, until the sugar has fully dissolved.

Bring to the boil, then turn down the heat and simmer for 2 minutes.

Remove from the heat and leave to cool for 10–15 minutes.

Meanwhile, soak the gelatine leaves in a bowl of cold water for 5 minutes.

Squeeze any excess water from the leaves and add to the glaze. Stir until fully dissolved.

Use a food thermometer to check the temperature of the glaze – make sure it has cooled to a maximum of 38°C before using.

"ANY HIGHER AND IT'S A NO-GO"

Pass your glaze through a sieve into a measuring jug to get rid of any bubbles.

Place your cake on a wire rack with a baking tray underneath and pour the glaze over the top of the cake, keeping an eye on the sides to make sure they are well covered. If you need more glaze, just pour the glaze that has been caught by the baking tray back through the sieve into the measuring jug and go again.

Put the cake in the fridge to firm up.

CARAMELISED HAZELNUTS

Measure the sugar and 1–2 tablespoons of water into a small pan over a medium heat. Do not stir. Just give it a swirl from time to time.

When the sugar is an amber caramel colour, remove the pan from the heat.

Attach each hazelnut to the end of a cocktail stick.

> "I CAN'T TELL YOU HOW MANY TIMES MUM HAS SHOUTED AT ME ABOUT THE CARAMEL FLOOR, SO ..."

Cover the floor and cupboards with newspaper or baking paper to protect them as the caramel will drip.

Very carefully dip each hazelnut into the caramel then hang them over the edge of a work surface, using tape or a heavy chopping board to hold the cocktail sticks in position. Caramel points will form as the caramel stretches.

Cut the points to the same length using scissors and remove from the cocktail sticks. Place on a sheet of baking paper until ready to use.

DÉCOR

Pipe small kisses of buttercream down the centre of the cake and place candied hazelnuts in between each kiss. Finish with some gold leaf.

BE CAREFUL, THE CARAMEL IS CRAZY HOT.

LET'S GO HALFIES

You can probably describe this recipe as a Valentine's Day special. Have you ever wanted a cake that's slightly bigger than a cupcake but daintier than a normal-sized cake? I designed these cakes to be shared. Like when you're at school or uni and one of your pals has a sandwich that's probably better than yours and you cheekily ask for a nibble or even half, if you dare. You should cut this cake right in half and share it over a film, cuppa or even dinner. It should go down a treat.

MAKES 6

Chocolate Sponge

175g plain flour
185g caster sugar
28g cocoa powder
½ tsp bicarbonate of soda
¼ tsp fine sea salt
75g dark chocolate chips
125ml buttermilk
125ml cold instant coffee
215ml vegetable oil
1½ large eggs
½ tsp vanilla extract

Coffee Cake

150g unsalted butter, cubed
150g golden caster sugar
75g light muscovado sugar
75g dark muscovado sugar
1½ large eggs
2 tbsp instant coffee
95ml soured cream
1½ tbsp vanilla extract
190g self-raising flour

Chocolate Sauce

50g dark chocolate (70% cocoa solids), broken into chunks
25g unsalted butter
125ml double cream
2 tbsp light brown sugar
1 tsp vanilla extract

You will need 12 × 8cm moulds and a blowtorch

Preheat oven to 180°C/Fan 160°C/Gas 4 and line the base of the moulds with baking paper.

Each cake uses 1½ eggs. To make the division easier, crack 3 eggs into a bowl, mix well, then put half in another bowl

CHOCOLATE CAKE

Sift your flour, sugar, cocoa powder, bicarbonate of soda and salt into a large bowl. Add your chocolate chips.

Combine your buttermilk, coffee, vegetable oil, eggs and vanilla in a separate bowl and give it a light whisk.

Add the dry ingredients to the wet ingredients in 3 batches, mixing well after each addition. Make sure you don't have any pockets of flour.

Divide the mixture evenly between 12 of the moulds – making sure you fill more than halfway – and place on baking trays in the oven. Bake for 20–25 minutes, until the sponges bounce back slightly when you press them gently.

Remove from the oven and allow to cool for 10–15 minutes in their moulds, before turning out on to a wire rack.

COFFEE CAKE

Measure the butter, sugars and 375ml of water into a large saucepan and place over a medium heat until the butter has melted.

Remove from the heat and allow to cool slightly.

Stir in the eggs, coffee, soured cream and vanilla extract.

Sift your flour into the pan and continue to stir until smooth.

Divide the mixture between 6 moulds – making sure you fill more than halfway. You may find you have enough mixture to fill a couple of extra moulds but that's not a problem in my book. Place the moulds on baking trays in the oven. Bake for 20–25 minutes, until a skewer inserted into the centre comes out clean.

Remove from the oven and allow to cool for 10–15 minutes in their moulds, before turning out on to a wire rack.

TURN OVER FOR MORE INGREDIENTS ⟶

Baileys Espresso Buttercream

300g unsalted butter, softened

650g icing sugar

3–4 tbsp espresso coffee

2 tbsp Baileys

½ tsp vanilla extract

Marshmallow Topping

1½ large egg whites

2½ tbsp golden syrup

100g caster sugar

¼ tsp cream of tartar

½ tsp fine sea salt

1 tbsp water

¾ tsp vanilla extract

½ tsp ground cinnamon

cocoa powder, for dusting

CHOCOLATE SAUCE

Melt the chocolate in a heatproof bowl using a bain-marie (see page 205), stirring occasionally, or in the microwave, heating in 20-second bursts.

Place all the other ingredients in a saucepan over a medium heat and stir gently until the sugar has dissolved.

Add this to the melted chocolate and stir until it's nice and smooth.

Remove from the heat and leave on one side to cool.

Once the sauce has reached room temperature, place it in the fridge and stir every 10 minutes.

BAILEYS ESPRESSO BUTTERCREAM

Beat your butter in a large bowl with a hand-held or free-standing mixer, until light and pale.

Sift your icing sugar into a separate bowl, then add it to the butter in 3 stages, beating after each addition. Scrape down the sides of the bowl from time to time.

Finally, add your espresso, Baileys and vanilla to loosen the buttercream.

MARSHMALLOW TOPPING

Combine the egg whites, golden syrup, sugar, cream of tartar, salt and water in a heatproof bowl and place over a bain-marie (see page 205). Beat with a hand-held whisk until stiff peaks are formed.

Remove from the heat, add the vanilla and cinnamon and whisk again.

ASSEMBLE

Trim all the chocolate and coffee sponges with a serrated knife so they're level.

Place the buttercream in a piping bag, cut off the tip and pipe kisses around the edge of each chocolate cake.

Place the chocolate sauce in another piping bag, cut off the tip and pipe this into the middle of the buttercream.

Sandwich a coffee sponge on top. Pipe another layer of kisses around the edge of the coffee cake and sandwich a chocolate sponge on top.

Place the marshmallow topping into a third piping bag with a round-tipped nozzle and pipe a good swirl of the marshmallow meringue over the chocolate sponge on top. Brown with a blowtorch then dust with cocoa powder.

Repeat with all the cakes until you have 6 to share.

MALTED CREPES

Question: how many pancakes do you have on Pancake Day? Shhh, you don't have to tell me but I have loads! You could probably stack them up into a multi-layered cake. That sounds like a plan! But, for it to be worthwhile, we gotta add a few extra trimmings … Fillings × flavours × crumb = the whole shebang.

SERVES 8

Pancakes
300g plain flour
2 tsp ground cinnamon
1 tsp fine sea salt
4 tbsp caster sugar
6 large eggs
900ml whole milk
1 tsp vanilla extract

Filling
500g mascarpone cheese
500g full-fat cream cheese
150g icing sugar, sifted
5 tbsp malt drink (10g malt powder × 80ml warm whole milk)
4 tbsp brandy
1 tsp vanilla extract
200ml double cream

To Fry and Serve
a couple knobs of butter, melted
a couple squiggles of vegetable oil
cocoa powder, to dust
4 × Would You Risk It For A … cookies (see page 171) or shop-bought chocolate chip cookies, half crumbled (optional)

I DARE YOU TO FLIP

Sift your flour, cinnamon, salt and sugar into a large bowl and mix with a whisk. Make a well right in the centre.

Crack in your eggs and mix until well combined.

Add the milk in a steady stream, mixing all the time.

Stir in the vanilla and your pancake mix is ready!

TIME TO FRY

Prepare a small bowl of melted butter and vegetable oil – you are going to use this to grease the pan between each pancake.

Place your pan over a medium heat and give it a good brush with your buttery oil.

Ladle some of your mixture into the pan – you want just enough to cover the base. Give the pan a good roll to spread the batter evenly.

Pop it back on the heat and cook for 2 minutes – BE ON THE WATCH.

Gently lift your pancake for a sneak peek – if it's golden brown it's cooked on that side.

Flip with a spatula and cook on the other side for 2 minutes. But, if you're feeling confident … you know what to do!

Remove the pancake from the heat and put on one side while you continue the pancake-making process, stacking them up as you go. Don't worry about them getting cold, it'll work to your advantage when decorating.

WHIP × SPREAD × STACK

Whisk the mascarpone, cream cheese, icing sugar, malt drink, brandy and vanilla in a large bowl with a hand-held mixer, until lighter and slightly thicker.

Add the double cream and whisk until it holds its shape.

Place one crepe on a serving board or plate and spread a little cream over the top with a palette knife. Top with another crepe and spread with more cream. Repeat the layers until all the crepes are used up.

Sprinkle the top with a generous amount of cocoa powder, finish with leftover cream and some crumbled chocolate chip cookies.

"YOU CAN MAKE THIS CREPE CAKE A DAY IN ADVANCE AND PLACE IT IN THE FRIDGE WITHOUT THE COCOA AND COOKIES. FINISH IT OFF THE NEXT MORNING AND BRING IT TO ROOM TEMPERATURE BEFORE SERVING. MY FAVOURITE PART ABOUT THIS BAKE IS ALL THOSE LAYERS."

COSY PANZONE

So, we all know about the traditional calzone, but what if we want one for breakfast, that is sweet and celebrates the pancake? Problem solved, mate. This fruity parcel is perfect on Pancake Day or as a breakfast-in-bed treat for someone special.

MAKES 6

Pancake Batter
100g plain flour
1 tsp ground cinnamon
¼ tsp fine sea salt
1 tbsp caster sugar
2 large eggs
300ml whole milk
¼ tsp vanilla extract

To Fry and Serve
a couple of knobs of butter, melted
a couple of squiggles of vegetable oil
½ quantity of Fruit Compote (see page 196)
your favourite yoghurt
icing sugar

FLIP, I DARE YOU

Sift your flour, cinnamon, salt and sugar into a large bowl and mix with a whisk. Make a well right in the centre.

Crack in your eggs and mix until well combined.

Add the milk in a steady stream, mixing all the time.

Stir in the vanilla and your pancake mix is ready!

TIME TO FRY

Prepare a small bowl of melted butter and vegetable oil – you are going to use this to grease the pan between each pancake.

Place your pan over a medium heat and give it a good brush with your buttery oil.

Ladle some of your mixture into the pan – you want just enough to cover the base. Give the pan a good roll to spread the batter evenly.

Pop it back on the heat and cook for 2 minutes – BE ON THE WATCH.

Gently lift your pancake for a sneak peak – if it's golden brown it's cooked on that side.

CALZONE TIME!

Give your one-side-cooked pancake a super-generous splat of the fruit compote and try to distribute it as evenly as possible.

Now, instead of giving your pancake the infamous 180° flip, you want to do a calzone fold. Lift one half of the pancake up and gently press it onto the other side, forming a semi-circle. Allow to cook for a couple more minutes.

Remove from the heat and place on one side, while you continue the calzone-making process. Carry on until all your pancake mixture is used up.

I LIKE TO SERVE THIS COMFORTING TREAT WITH GOOD GREEK OR VANILL YOGHURT AND A SPRINK OF ICING SUGAR.

19

This was the year Mum thought it would be clever to go on holiday … during my birthday. Every year without fail she had always sorted out my cake – the best ones – but not this time. So I just said to myself, "I'm gonna make my own birthday cake." Inspired by some of my favourite things to bake, it is six layers of brown butter banana sponge × almond butter × granola cheesecake filling.

SERVES 24-30

Brown Butter Banana Sponge

1kg unsalted butter (you need 750g brown butter), cubed

600g caster sugar

150g light brown sugar

12 eggs

840g self-raising flour

½ tsp baking powder

2 tsp mixed spice

90ml whole milk

1 tsp vanilla extract

3 large bananas, mashed

Yoghurt Cheesecake Filling

300g full-fat cream cheese

300g Greek yoghurt

300g icing sugar

250g double cream

1 tsp vanilla extract

Almond Butter Buttercream

900g unsalted butter, softened

270g almond butter, softened

1.95kg icing sugar

150–180ml whole milk

1 tbsp vanilla extract

Filling and Décor

250g granola

You will need 6 × 20cm cake tins (if you don't have 6 make the sponges in batches)

BURN THE BUTTER

You may want to do this the day before. Place the butter in a saucepan over a medium heat and melt until the milk solids have almost burnt and it has turned a deep amber colour.

Pour the butter into a container to cool. You may see little black bits at the bottom of the saucepan, you want that in your butter – that's where the flavour is!

Once cool, put in the fridge.

Preheat oven to 180°C/Fan 160°C/Gas 4 and grease and line the cake tins.

FOR THE CAKE

Measure 750g browned butter and both sugars into a large bowl and beat with a hand-held or free-standing mixer until light and fluffy.

Crack in the eggs one at a time, mixing after each addition. If the mixture begins to curdle just add a couple of tablespoons of the flour and it should bring it back together.

Turn the speed down very low and add your flour, baking powder and mixed spice.

Add the milk, vanilla and bananas to loosen the mixture.

Continue to mix on low speed until everything comes together. You may want to scrape down the sides of the bowl to make sure everything is well mixed.

> "THE WORST THING IS TO FIND SMALL POCKETS OF FLOUR."

Divide the mixture evenly between the tins and bake for 25–27 minutes, until a skewer poked into the middle comes out clean.

CHEESECAKE FILLING

Lightly whip the cream cheese and Greek yoghurt together in a large bowl using a hand-held mixer.

Sift your icing sugar into the bowl and beat until smooth.

Stir in the double cream – it should be a spreadable consistency.

Add your vanilla and beat again.

Place a sheet of clingfilm over the bowl and pop in the fridge until needed.

TURN OVER ⟹

ALMOND BUTTER BUTTERCREAM

Beat the butter and almond butter together in a large bowl with a hand-held or free-standing mixer on a medium–high setting for 5–8 minutes, until light and fluffy.

Sift your icing sugar into a separate bowl and add to the butter mixture in 2 batches, beating for 7–8 minutes after each addition.

Add your milk and vanilla to loosen the buttercream and beat again for a further 3 minutes, until light and fluffy.

CAKE ... ASSEMBLE!

Use a cake leveller or sharp knife to trim the top off all the cakes so they are level.

Spread a small amount of buttercream on a board that is slightly bigger than your sponges and place your first layer of sponge on top. Place that board on a turntable, if you have one.

Fill two piping bags – one with half the buttercream and the other with the cheesecake filling – and have your granola at the ready. Cut the tip off both piping bags and, while rotating the turntable, pipe a buttercream border around the sponge leaving an 8cm circle in the middle. Fill that circle with cheesecake filling and finish with a generous sprinkle of granola.

Place another layer of banana sponge on top and repeat the filling. Continue until all the cakes are stacked, making sure your last sponge is placed upside down on top.

Using a palette knife, cake scraper and a turntable, coat the sides and top of the cake with a thin layer of buttercream until it's covered.

Place your cake in the fridge for at least an hour to set.

IT'S A PRETTY TALL CAKE BUT WHO CARES? IT WAS MY BIRTHDAY!

DÉCOR

Place the other half of the buttercream in the piping bag and apply a final layer of buttercream around and on top of the cake.

Now, I admit almond butter is a little bit of a hipster ingredient so we're going to make it even more hipster by adding texture to the outside of the cake. Using a miniature offset palette knife and, starting from the bottom of the cake, gently press the tip of the knife into the final coat of buttercream, rotating the turntable at the same time. Gradually move up the cake and it should result in a pretty banging rippled effect.

Use the leftover buttercream to pipe around the top edges of the cake with a large nozzle of your choice.

Finally, sprinkle with that granola, baby!

TRICK OR CHEEKY TREAT

When you go to your next Halloween house party, bring this along, trust me!

SERVES 16–24

Pumpkin Sponge

4 large eggs

250ml vegetable oil

300g pumpkin purée

250g self-raising flour

2 tsp mixed spice

1 tsp ground cinnamon

½ nutmeg, grated

1 tsp bicarbonate of soda

250g light muscovado sugar

1 tsp vanilla extract

Chocolate Guinness Cake

250ml Guinness

250g unsalted butter, cubed

75g cocoa powder

400g caster sugar

142ml soured cream

2 large eggs

1 tbsp vanilla extract

280g plain flour

2½ tsp bicarbonate of soda

Chai Buttercream

250ml whole milk

6 tsp chai latte powder

600g unsalted butter, softened

1.3kg icing sugar

Decorations

6 Oreos, crushed

180g white marshmallows

You will need 4 × 20cm cake tins

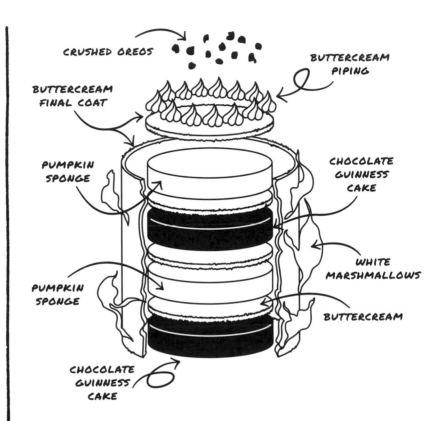

CRUSHED OREOS

BUTTERCREAM PIPING

BUTTERCREAM FINAL COAT

PUMPKIN SPONGE

CHOCOLATE GUINNESS CAKE

PUMPKIN SPONGE

WHITE MARSHMALLOWS

BUTTERCREAM

CHOCOLATE GUINNESS CAKE

Preheat oven to 180°C/Fan 160°C/Gas 4 and grease and line the cake tins with baking paper.

START WITH THE PUMPKIN CAKE

Crack the eggs into a large bowl and whisk.

Add the vegetable oil and whisk again.

Tip in the pumpkin purée and whisk once more.

Sift your flour, spices and bicarbonate of soda into a separate bowl, add the sugar and stir.

Add the dry ingredients to the wet ingredients with the vanilla and whisk until they are well incorporated.

Divide the mixture evenly between two of the tins and bake for 25–27 minutes, until a skewer inserted into the middle of the cake comes out clean.

Remove from the oven and allow to cool for 15 minutes in the tins before turning out on to a wire rack.

TURN OVER ⟹

NOW THE CHOCOLATE CAKE

Pour the Guinness into a large saucepan and place over a medium heat.

Add the butter and leave to melt.

Remove from the heat and whisk in the cocoa powder and sugar.

Beat the soured cream in a large bowl with a hand-held or free-standing mixer.

Crack in the eggs, one at a time, mixing after each addition, then stir in the vanilla.

Pour the soured cream mixture into the Guinness mixture and stir.

Finally, stir in your flour and bicarbonate of soda.

Divide the mixture evenly between the two remaining tins and bake for 25–30 minutes, until a skewer inserted into the middle of the cake comes out clean.

Remove from the oven and allow to cool for 15 minutes in the tins before turning out on to a wire rack.

CRACK ON WITH THE BUTTERCREAM

Pour your milk into a small saucepan. Add the chai latte powder and place over a medium heat. Stir and bring just to the boil.

Remove from the heat and place on one side to cool.

Measure the butter into a large bowl and, using a hand-held or free-standing mixer, beat the butter until light and fluffy.

Sift your icing sugar into a separate bowl, then add to the butter in 3 stages, beating after each addition. Scrape down the sides of the bowl from time to time.

Add 1–2 tablespoons of your chai latte milk to loosen the buttercream.

LAYER * CRUMB * FINAL COAT

Use a cake leveller or sharp knife to trim the top off all the cakes so they are level.

Spread a small amount of buttercream on a board that is slightly bigger than your sponges and place your first layer of Guinness sponge on top. Place that board on a turntable, if you have one.

Place half the buttercream into a piping bag with a round-tipped nozzle. Pipe a thin layer of buttercream on the first sponge then place a pumpkin sponge on top. Repeat and alternate the sponges, making sure your last sponge is placed upside down on top.

Using a palette knife, cake scraper and a turntable, coat the sides and top of the cake with a thin layer of buttercream until it's covered.

Place your cake in the fridge for at least an hour to set.

Place the other half of the buttercream into a piping bag. Take the cake out of the fridge and apply another layer of buttercream around and on top of the cake.

Use the leftover buttercream to pipe around the top edges of your cake.

DÉCOR

Sprinkle the cake with crushed Oreos and stick it back in the fridge.

"WE AIN'T DONE YET – WHAT'S HALLOWEEN WITHOUT THE WEBS?"

Melt the marshmallows in a heatproof bowl in the microwave in 30-second bursts, stirring occasionally.

Remove your cake from the fridge.

Touch two fingertips together and dip them into the marshmallow, then remove your fingers and stretch them apart – you'll create stretchy strands of marshmallow.

Wrap them around your cake but don't be hesitant or it'll look weird.

GO FOR IT!

PDP (PRE-DINNER PIES)

We tend to have pies for dessert on Christmas Day – cough, mince pies, cough –
but having a pie for starters or even as a snack? Hmmmm … let's have a go.

MAKES 24

Herby Shortcrust

700g plain flour
1 tbsp freshly chopped thyme
1 tbsp freshly chopped rosemary
1 tsp fine sea salt
400g unsalted butter, cold, cubed
4 large eggs
2 tbsp cold water

Brie and Turkey Filling

4 boneless skinless turkey breasts
2 tbsp vinegar
juice of 1 lemon
1 tsp fine sea salt
1 tsp cracked black pepper
3 tsp mixed herbs
2 tbsp olive oil
all-purpose seasoning, by eye
8 pancetta strips
300g Brie, cubed

Cranberry Sauce

150g light brown sugar
150ml fresh orange juice
2 tbsp cornflour
4 tbsp water
375g frozen cranberries
zest of 1 orange
1 tbsp grated fresh root ginger
1 cinnamon stick

Mashed Potato

1kg Maris Piper potatoes
50g unsalted butter
fine sea salt, to taste
black pepper, to taste
100ml whole milk
100g Brie, cubed and rind cut off

**You will need 2 × 12-hole
muffin trays and a blowtorch
(optional)**

PASTRY

Tip the flour, thyme, rosemary, salt and
butter into a food-processor and pulse
until it resembles fine breadcrumbs.

Crack 2 of the eggs into a bowl with the
cold water and beat lightly.

While the motor is running, add the
egg and water mixture and pulse until it
starts to come together into a ball.

Tip the pastry on to a lightly floured
work surface and gently bring it together.

Divide the dough into a quarter and
three quarters. Wrap both balls in
clingfilm and place in the fridge to chill.

SAUCE

Time to prepare the cranberry sauce. Tip
the sugar and orange juice into a large
saucepan, place over a medium heat and
bring to the boil.

Mix the cornflour and water in a small
bowl, and add this to the pan.

Tip in the cranberries, orange zest, ginger
and cinnamon stick, turn down the heat
and simmer for 5–10 minutes. You want
the cranberries to hold their shape, so
keep an eye out.

Remove from the heat and leave to cool.
It will thicken up, trust me.

Place in the fridge until ready to use.

SEASON UP ×
COOK UP

Preheat oven to 180°C/Fan 160°C/Gas 4.

Place the turkey in a bowl with the
salt, pepper, mixed herbs, olive oil and
all-purpose seasoning, to taste. Massage
your meat. Take care of it! Leave it to
stand for a couple of minutes. (You can
do this a day in advance and it will taste
better. If you do, place clingfilm over the
top and leave in the fridge overnight.)

Place the turkey on a baking tray, cover
with foil and bake for 20 minutes, until
the juices run clear. Remove from the
oven and leave to cool.

Turn the oven temperature up to 200°C/
Fan 180°C/Gas 6 and place two baking
trays in the oven to heat up.

LEFTOVER CRANBERRY SAUCE CAN BE USED IN YOUR CHRISTMAS LUNCH.

TURN OVER ⟶

FINISH THE FILLING

Place the pancetta in a large frying pan over a medium-high heat and cook for 3–5 minutes on each side. This will render the fat and make it super crispy – my mate told me this.

Remove from the heat and place the pancetta on kitchen paper to absorb the excess oil.

Cut the pancetta into small pieces and chop the cold turkey into smallish cubes. Tip them both into a large bowl. Add a few heaped tablespoons of cranberry sauce and stir.

Finally, add the chunks of Brie and give it one more stir. Place on one side until ready to use.

ROLL × CUT × FILL 'EM UP

Get your large piece of pastry out of the fridge and roll out on a lightly floured surface into a large rectangle the thickness of a £1 coin. Stamp out 24 × 10cm circles and place them into the muffin trays.

Fill the cases with the Christmassy filling.

Re-roll the off-cuts of pastry and the spare quarter to the thickness of a £1 coin. Cut 24 × 7cm circles and use these to top the pies – press to seal.

Lightly beat the remaining 2 eggs to make an egg wash and use to brush the pastry tops. Place the muffin trays on the hot baking trays in the oven and bake for 20 minutes, until golden brown.

Remove from the oven and leave to cool in their tins for 10–15 minutes, then carefully pop each pie out of its tray and place on a wire rack.

MASH POTATO

Meanwhile, peel and chop the potatoes into similar-sized chunks, then tip into a large pot of boiling salted water. Cook over a medium heat for 20 minutes until tender.

Drain the potatoes and leave in a colander to steam dry.

Pop the potatoes back into the pan and mash well.

Add half your butter, the salt and pepper, and mash again, adding a couple of splashes of milk to loosen.

Finish with the remaining butter, milk and Brie, then mash again.

Spoon the potato into a piping bag with a large nozzle and pipe the mash on top of the pies in two rings.

As the finishing touch, grill the tops of the pies. Either preheat the grill to a medium–high heat and brown the pies underneath it for 5 minutes, or use a blowtorch on the piped mash.

Drizzle with some cranberry sauce and BOSH!

IT'S CHRISTMAS AFTER ALL

Promise me you'll only make this festive cheesecake on Christmas Eve.
I mean it or, or . . . or else all your Christmas dinner will taste like Brussels sprouts!

SERVES 12

Chocolate × Orange × Cranberry Shortbread

340g unsalted butter, softened

165g golden caster sugar

340g plain flour, plus extra for dusting

165g cornflour

zest of 3 oranges

2 tsp mixed spice

1 tbsp vanilla extract

200g dark chocolate (70% cocoa solids), broken into chunks

200g dried cranberries

Mince Pie Cream Cheese

900g full-fat cream cheese

200g caster sugar

200ml soured cream

3 tbsp plain flour

3 free-range eggs plus 1 yolk, lightly beaten

2 tsp vanilla extract

450g mincemeat

Chocolate Bark × Baileys Cream

300g dark chocolate (70% cocoa solids), broken into chunks

100g dried cranberries, roughly chopped

zest of 2 oranges

300ml double cream

2 tbsp caster sugar

2 tsp vanilla extract

Baileys, to taste

You will need a 23cm springform cake tin

Preheat oven to 180°C/Fan 160°C/Gas 4 and grease and line the base of the tin.

START YOUR SHORTBREAD

Cream your butter and sugar together in a large bowl with a free-standing or hand-held mixer until light and fluffy.

Add your flour and cornflour, orange zest, mixed spice and vanilla. Mix until the dough is just coming together, then chuck in your chocolate and cranberries.

Place the dough on a lightly floured surface and knead gently – do not go crazy! Wrap in clingfilm and place in the fridge for 20 minutes.

CRACK ON WITH YOUR FILLING

Beat the cream cheese and sugar together in a large bowl with a hand-held or free-standing mixer until creamy.

Measure your soured cream and plain flour into the bowl and mix again.

Crack the eggs in one at a time, beating after each addition, until well combined.

Finally, add your vanilla and (this is where it gets exciting!) the mincemeat.

Cover the bowl with clingfilm and place in the fridge until needed.

ROLL × CUT × BAKE

Take the dough out of the fridge and roll out on a lightly floured surface to the thickness of two £1 coins. Cut out a 23cm circle and place it in the base of the springform tin.

Place on a baking tray and bake for 20 minutes, until light golden brown.

Remove from the oven and place on a wire rack to cool.

Drop your oven temperature to 150°C/Fan 130°C/Gas 2.

YOU'RE GOING TO HAVE LEFTOVER SHORTBREAD DOUGH SO THIS IS THE PERFECT TIME TO ROLL, CUT AND BAKE SOME CHRISTMAS TREE BISCUITS. SOUNDS LIKE A PLAN, NO?

TURN OVER ⟹

CHEESECAKE TIME

Pour your cheesecake mixture on to the biscuit base and return to the oven to bake for 1 hour. You're looking for it to have a cheeky little wobble in the middle.

Switch off the oven and leave to cool in the oven for 30 minutes with the door slightly ajar.

Remove from the oven and leave on the side to cool completely.

Place in the fridge for at least 1 hour to chill, or preferably overnight.

CHOCOLATE BARK

While the cheesecake is chilling, it's time for DÉCOR!

Melt the chocolate in a heatproof bowl over a bain-marie (see page 205) stirring occasionally, or in a microwave, heating in 20-second bursts.

Line a baking tray with baking paper then pour in the chocolate. Scatter over the cranberries and orange zest and place in the fridge to set.

Remove from the fridge and break into funky and pointy shapes.

BAILEYS CREAM

Meanwhile, whip the double cream, sugar and vanilla in a large bowl until it's just whipped, in soft peaks.

Now, the amount of Baileys you use should really be determined on the day – Monday, 1 tablespoon, Friday to Sunday, well, it's entirely up to you. Add the Baileys and continue to whip, until medium peaks are formed.

SERVE UP

Pop out the cheesecake and place it on a large serving plate or display board.

Smother the top in wavy clouds of Baileys cream and stand chocolate bark shards up in the cream.

SLICE UP AND ENJOY.

MERRY CHRISTMAS!

MINCE PIE BLONDIES

All right, I love mince pies, but try adding your festive mincemeat into another bake. Mince pie blondie anyone?

MAKES ABOUT 15 PIECES

250g unsalted butter, cubed
420g light soft brown sugar
3 large eggs
1½ tbsp vanilla extract
330g plain flour
1½ tsp baking powder
1 tsp fine sea salt
2 tbsp mixed spice
1 tsp ground cinnamon
1 tsp ground cloves
zest of 2 oranges
400g mincemeat

You will need a 28 × 33cm baking tray

BROWN THAT BUTTER

Place the butter in a saucepan over a medium heat and melt until the milk solids have almost burnt and it has turned a deep amber colour.

Remove from the heat and pour into a large bowl to cool.

Preheat oven to 190°C/Fan 170°C/Gas 5 and grease and line the baking tray with baking paper.

BLONDIE × BAKE

Add the sugar to the melted brown butter, then crack in the eggs one at a time, stirring after each addition.

Stir in the vanilla.

Tip in the flour, baking powder, salt, spices and orange zest and begin to fold.

Finally, stir in your mincemeat.

Tip the blondie mixture into the baking tray and spread evenly. Bake for 25–30 minutes, until golden brown.

Remove from the oven and leave in the tray until completely cool.

SERVE IN CHUNKS WITH HUGE SCOOPS OF ICE CREAM, CUSTARD OR FORGET THE ADD-ONS AND EAT IT BY ITSELF.

Simple

BREKKY MUFFINS

You're on the go but breakfast is essential. Before you leave the house you take a last glance at your kitchen worktop and you see cupcakes and a fruit and nut mixture – what do you choose? How about a combination of the two?

MAKES 24

450g self-raising flour
1½ tsp baking powder
¼ tsp ground cloves
1 tsp ground cinnamon
150g light brown sugar
75g dark brown sugar
3 large eggs
375ml whole milk
150g unsalted butter, melted
½ tsp vanilla extract
100g mixed dried fruit
160g pecans, toasted and chopped

You will need 2 × 12-hole muffin trays and 24 cupcake cases

Preheat oven to 180°C/Fan 160°C/Gas 4 and line the muffin trays with cupcake cases.

MUFFIN MIX

Sift your flour, baking powder, cloves and cinnamon into a large bowl and stir in both sugars.

Whisk your eggs, milk, butter and vanilla in a separate bowl.

Tip the wet ingredients into the dry and quickly mix together.

Stir in your dried fruit and pecans.

BAKE 'EM

Fill each paper case just over halfway and bake for 23 minutes, until a skewer inserted into the middle of a muffin comes out clean.

> "I KNOW, WHY SO PRECISE? BUT IT ALWAYS SEEMS TO WORK FOR ME. GIVE IT A COUPLE MORE MINUTES THOUGH, IF THEY ARE NOT BAKED."

Allow to cool for a couple of minutes before you nab one and dart out the door.

"NEVER RUN OUT OF BARS"

Rapper Chip once said that he can't run out of bars – and neither can I! Whether for breakfast or just a snack, these bars are massive crowd-pleasers. Once your pals taste these, you know they'll be coming back for more.

HEALTHY NUT BARS

MAKES ABOUT 15

100g blanched almonds, roughly chopped

75g unsalted butter

3 tbsp Classic Smooth (see page 199) or shop-bought smooth peanut butter

5 tbsp runny honey

3 ripe bananas, mashed

2 Granny Smith apples, peeled, cored and grated

375g rolled oats

½ tsp ground cinnamon

150g raisins

100g dark chocolate (70% cocoa solids), broken into chunks

You will need a 20 × 30cm high-lipped baking tin

Preheat oven 180°C/Fan 160°C/Gas 4. Grease and line the baking tin with baking paper and line a separate baking tray with baking paper.

ALMOND TOASTING

Tip your almonds on to the baking tray and spread out. Bake for 15 minutes, giving them a good stir halfway through.

Remove from the oven and leave to cool.

Drop the oven temperature to 160°C/Fan 140°C/Gas 3.

CRACK ON WITH THE BAR

Measure the butter, peanut butter and honey into a saucepan and place over a medium heat until melted.

Remove from the heat and add the banana, apples and 150ml of water from the kettle. Give it a good mix.

> "YOU PRETTY MUCH WANT TO SQUASH IT SO WHEN YOU CUT THE BARS THEY ARE WELL COMPACT ... I USE A POTATO MASHER – MOST OF THEM ARE AT A 90° ANGLE, SO YOU CAN GET A LEVEL SURFACE."

Chuck your oats, cinnamon, raisins and toasted almonds into a large bowl and pour in the mixture from the saucepan. Give it a good stir to make sure everything is well coated.

Tip into the baking tin and level it out.

Bake for 1 hour, until golden brown.

Remove from the oven and leave it to cool in the tin.

CHOCOLATE TOP

Melt your chocolate in a heatproof bowl over a bain-marie (see page 205) or in the microwave, heating in 20-second bursts.

Use a spoon to give your bar a squiggle of the chocolate, then leave to set and slice into portions.

VEGAN FLAPJACKS

MAKES ABOUT 15

310g Medjool dates, stoned

200g low-fat soya spread

7 tbsp agave syrup

150g dried apricots, finely chopped

100g pecans, toasted and chopped

6 tbsp mixed seeds

120g raisins

300g porridge oats

You will need a 20 × 30cm high-lipped baking tin

Preheat oven to 190°C/Fan 170°C/Gas 5 and line the baking tin with baking paper.

Tip the dates into a food-processor and whizz. You want them to be finely chopped and pretty much stick together in clumps.

Place the low-fat soya spread, agave syrup and dates in a large saucepan over a gentle heat and stir until the spread has melted and the dates are well mixed.

Remove from the heat and add all the remaining ingredients. Stir until everything is mixed well.

Spoon the mixture into the tin, level it out and bake for 35–40 minutes.

Remove from the oven and leave to cool in the tin before cutting into generous wedges.

Store in an airtight container ready for daily munchies.

OH, HOW CHEESY

Let's be honest, everyone's been through the phase of making
cheese toasties … But this isn't any old toastie, it's on a whole new level.
A generous spread of that maple butter gives you the perfect combo
of sweet and salty. Do you know what would be mad, though? Heating up
some tomato soup and using it as a dip. Go on, I dare you.

SERVES 1

3 rashers smoked streaky bacon

2 slices thick white bread

Maple Butter

15g salted butter, softened

1 tsp maple syrup

Cheeses

25g mature Cheddar, grated

25g Gruyère, grated

25g hard mozzarella, grated

MAPLE BUTTER

Place the ingredients in a small bowl and
beat until thoroughly combined. Leave to
one side until ready to use.

> "I USUALLY MAKE A
> BIG BATCH OF MAPLE
> BUTTER AND KEEP
> IT IN THE FRIDGE
> FOR ALL MY TOASTIE
> NEEDS."

STREAKY BACON

Place the bacon in a large frying pan over
a medium heat and fry for 3–5 minutes
each side to render the fat and make it
super crispy.

Remove from the heat and place the
bacon on some kitchen paper to drain
the excess oil.

Chop into small pieces and place in a
bowl with the grated cheese. Give it a
good mix.

ASSEMBLE × FRY

Spread the maple butter on both sides
of your bread. Give one slice a generous
sprinkle of the bacon cheese, then top
with the other slice.

Place a frying pan over a low to medium
heat and cook the bad boy for 3–4
minutes, until golden brown, pressing
down with a spatula.

> "FLIP! BUT NOT LIKE
> A PANCAKE."

Cook on the other side for a further
3–4 minutes.

Remove from the heat and place on a
plate with a spoonful of chutney on the
side – whichever takes your fancy.

Leave to cool for a couple of minutes,
because it's going to be piping hot, then
cut in half, and share it with yourself.

DUNK,
CRUMBLE,
YUM.

BISCUITS

WOULD YOU RISK IT FOR A . . .?

Ayyy you know what I'm going to say, the lyrics to one of my all-time bangers, "Frisky" by Tinie Tempah. It had to become a recipe.

MAKES 20-25

250g unsalted butter, softened

70g granulated sugar

70g light muscovado sugar

2 tsp vanilla extract

300g plain flour

1 tsp fine sea salt

1 tsp bicarbonate of soda

100g milk chocolate, chopped into small pieces

100g dark chocolate (70% cocoa solids), chopped into small pieces

Preheat oven to 180°C/Fan 160°C/ Gas 4 and line two baking trays with baking paper.

COOKIE TIME

Cream the butter and both sugars together in a large bowl, using a hand-held or free-standing mixer, until light and fluffy.

Add the vanilla and mix again.

Sift your flour, salt and bicarbonate of soda into a separate bowl, then add to the butter mixture, mixing well.

Stir in the chocolate chips and mix again.

BAKING TIME

Using an ice-cream scoop, place portions of the cookie dough on your baking trays and bake for 12–15 minutes.

> "LEAVE LOTS OF SPACE BETWEEN THEM AS THEY SPREAD OUT A LOT DURING BAKING."

Remove from the oven and leave to firm up on the baking trays before transferring to a wire rack to cool.

CUSTARD STAMPS

This is my take on a classic and favourite — the custard cream. Have one with milk, a cuppa, or you can even crumble these over ice cream …What do you fancy?

MAKES 20–25

250g unsalted butter, softened

140g golden caster sugar

1 large egg yolk

2 tsp vanilla extract

250g plain flour, plus extra for dusting

1 tsp fine sea salt

50g custard powder

Buttercream

150g unsalted butter, softened

325g icing sugar

60ml whole milk

½ tsp vanilla extract

You will need a 5cm square crinkle-edged cutter

FOR THE BISCUIT

Cream the butter and sugar together in a large bowl with a hand-held or free-standing mixer until it's well incorporated but not fluffy. You don't want too much air in the biscuit dough.

Add the egg yolk and vanilla and mix.

Sift your dry ingredients into the bowl and continue to mix until it's just combined.

Tip the dough on a lightly floured surface and bring together.

Wrap in clingfilm and pop in the fridge for at least 20 minutes while you sort out your buttercream.

BUTTERCREAM

Beat your butter in a large bowl with a hand-held or free-standing mixer, until light and pale.

Sift your icing sugar into a separate bowl, then add it to the butter in 3 stages, beating after each addition. Scrape down the sides of the bowl from time to time.

Finally, add your milk and vanilla to loosen the buttercream.

ROLL × CUT × BAKE

Preheat oven to 180°C/Fan 160°C/Gas 4 and line three baking trays with baking paper.

Take the dough out of the fridge and cut it in half so it's easier to handle. Roll each half out on a lightly floured surface to the thickness of a £1 coin. Cut out your squares, preferably with a crinkle-edged 5cm square cutter.

Place on the baking trays and bake for 10–12 minutes, until golden brown.

Remove from the oven and leave to firm up on the trays before transferring to a wire rack to finish cooling.

FLIP × PIPE × SANDWICH

Flip half of the biscuits over and add a generous dollop of buttercream. Sandwich another biscuit on top.

There we have it: CUSTARD STAMPS!

PROPER DUNKERS

Now these biscuits are definitely double … triple … quadruple … quintruple … alright, I'll stop there … proper dunkers.

MAKES 25-30

165g unsalted butter, cold, cubed
225g plain wholemeal flour
225g coarse or medium oatmeal
80g light brown sugar
100g raisins
1 tsp white wine vinegar
100ml whole milk
20g runny honey
1 tsp bicarbonate of soda
200g dark chocolate (70% cocoa solids), broken into chunks

You will need a 7cm cutter

MAKE

Place the butter in a large bowl with the flour, oatmeal and sugar. Rub the mixture with your fingertips until it resembles breadcrumbs.

Tip in your raisins and stir.

Combine the vinegar, milk, honey and bicarbonate of soda in a separate bowl and give it a good mix.

Add the wet ingredients to the dry and mix until it forms a workable dough.

Wrap in clingfilm and leave to chill in the fridge for a couple of hours.

BAKE

Preheat oven to 140°C/Fan 120°C/Gas 1 and line two baking trays with baking paper.

Take the dough out of the fridge and let it soften for 10 minutes.

Roll out on a lightly floured surface to a thickness of 5mm. Cut circles using a 7cm cutter and place them on the baking trays.

You should have about 25–30 biscuits. Bake for 25 minutes, until golden brown.

Remove from the oven and leave to firm up on the trays before transferring to a wire rack to finish cooling.

FINISH

Melt the chocolate in a heatproof bowl using a bain-marie (see page 205), or in the microwave, heating in 20-second bursts, stirring after each one.

Dip the cooled biscuits in the melted chocolate and place back on the wire rack to set.

YOU KNOW THE DEAL - RE-ROLL AND KEEP ON CUTTING.

CRANBERRY ✳ CASHEW ✳ WHITE CHOCOLATE BISCUITS

Before I baked, when Mum used to do our Sunday shop, our favourite part was the much-anticipated biscuit aisle. We'd always get a good variety of biscuits but one that never failed to make it into the basket was a crumbly, short-textured cookie. They were always on the top shelf and back then I was only 4-foot something, so you see my problem? Anyway, there's me waffling again … These cookies are packed with white chocolate, roasted cashew nuts and dried cranberries. They're slightly addictive but that's okay — a cookie a day keeps the … Hmmm, I'm gonna have to think about that one!

MAKES 20–25

180g unsalted butter, softened
90g golden caster sugar
1 tsp vanilla extract
225g plain flour
80g cashew nuts, toasted
80g dried cranberries
100g white chocolate, chopped into small pieces

Preheat oven to 180°C/Fan 160°C/Gas 4 and line a large baking tray with baking paper.

DOUGH

Cream the butter, sugar and vanilla together in a large bowl with a hand-held or free-standing mixer until it's approaching creamy.

Tip in the flour, cashews, cranberries and chocolate and bring it together to form a dough.

"GET YOUR HANDS STUCK IN."

Divide the dough in two and shape each half into a log with a 5cm diameter.

Wrap them both in clingfilm and pop in the fridge to chill for an hour.

BAKE

Take the dough out of the fridge and slice into discs, each 1cm thick. Place them on the baking tray and bake for 15 minutes.

Let the biscuits firm up on the tray then transfer to a wire rack to cool.

CHOCOLATE × PEANUT × BACON SARNIES

Sweet but with savoury notes – and it's all done in a food-processor! Dishes for washing kept to a minimum – whoop, whoop! If you don't have a food-processor, you can achieve the same result by hand, it'll just take slightly longer.

MAKES 15–16

Candied Bacon

100g soft light brown sugar
8 rashers smoked streaky bacon

Chocolate Biscuits

155g icing sugar
1 tsp fine sea salt
225g unsalted butter, softened
300g plain flour, sifted
50g cocoa powder, sifted

Buttercream

300g icing sugar, sifted
100g unsalted butter, softened
50g Classic Smooth (see page 199) or shop-bought smooth peanut butter
60ml whole milk
30g pretzels, finely ground

Preheat oven to 190°C/Fan 170°C/Gas 5 and line a baking tray with foil.

CANDY YOUR BACON

Rub your soft brown sugar on the bacon and place on the baking tray.

Cook for 10 minutes then flip the bacon on to the other side and bake for a further 5 minutes.

Remove from the oven and let the bacon cool.

Chop into small chunky pieces.

DOUGH × ROLL

Tip all the ingredients for the biscuits into a food-processor and mix until it comes together. If it doesn't quite form a dough, you can tip it out on a lightly floured surface and bring it together.

Form the dough into a log with a 5cm diameter, wrap in clingfilm and pop in the fridge to chill for 1 hour.

BUTTERCREAM

Meanwhile, pop all the ingredients for the buttercream except for the pretzels into the food-processor and mix to a smooth and creamy consistency. If it's a little stiff, splash in a bit more milk.

Finally, fold in the pretzels.

BAKE

Preheat oven to 140°C/Fan 120°C/Gas 2 and line two baking trays with baking paper.

Take the dough out of the fridge and cut into 30–32 discs, each 5mm thick. Place them on the baking trays and bake for 25 minutes.

> "SOMETIMES I JUST WANT TO SAY ... BAKE UNTIL IT LOOKS TASTY!"

Remove from the oven and leave to firm up on the trays before transferring to a wire rack to finish cooling.

SARNIES

Flip half the biscuits onto their backs and pipe an even disc of buttercream on top, followed by a few pieces of bacon. Use your remaining biscuits to sandwich them up.

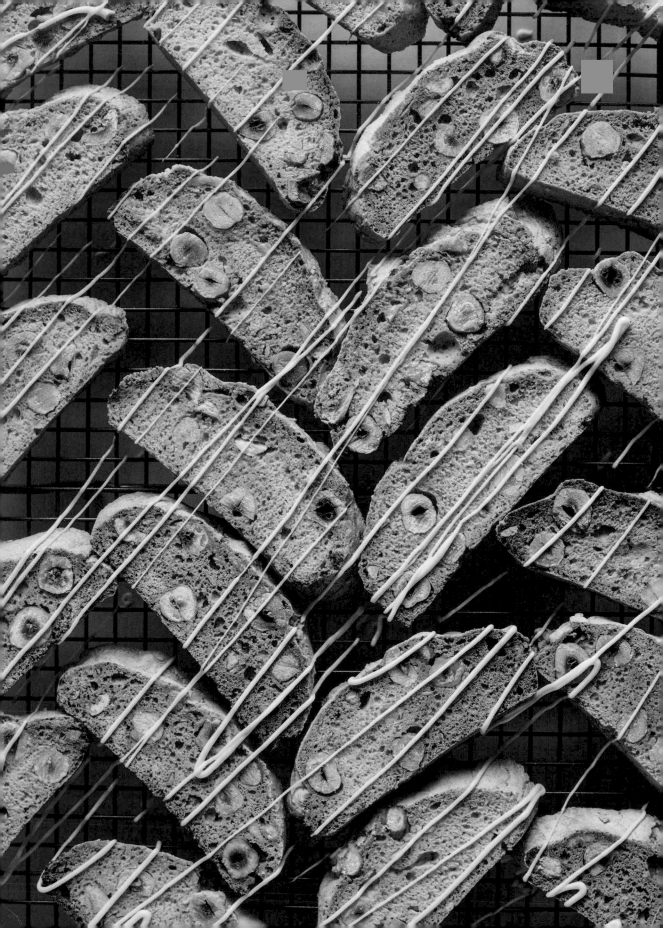

WHITE LIME HAZELNUT BISCOTTI

I remember the first time I baked these classic biscuits, I instantly loved making them. The possibilities of flavour combinations are endless.

MAKES 20-25

250g plain flour, plus extra for dusting
½ tsp baking powder
250g caster sugar
3 medium eggs, beaten
200g hazelnuts
finely grated zest of 2 limes
100g white chocolate, melted

Preheat oven to 170°C/Fan 150°C/ Gas 3 and line a large baking tray with baking paper.

Mix the flour, baking powder and sugar in a large bowl and crack in the eggs. Bring together slowly to make a dough.

Add the hazelnuts and lime zest and knead the dough gently on a lightly floured surface, then divide into two. Roll each half into a log about 30cm long.

BAKE TAKE ONE

Place on the baking tray and bake for 25–27 minutes.

Remove from the oven, leave to cool slightly, then cut each log into 2cm slices. Lay the slices back on the baking tray.

BAKE TAKE TWO

Pop the tray back in the oven for a further 8 minutes.

Turn the biscotti over and bake for another 8 minutes, until golden brown.

Remove from the oven and leave to firm on the tray before placing on a wire rack to cool.

CHOC ON TOP

Line all the biscotti up and, using a spoon, give them a good squiggle with the melted white chocolate.

Leave for a while to set, then enjoy.

DEFINITELY GOING ON THE MENU

Banana bread is such a crowd pleaser and is extremely versatile – chuck in a few nuts, chocolate chips, fold in some fresh blueberries, you name it. When I came up with this recipe I said to myself, "If I ever open a shop, café or a pop-up this will be … definitely going on the menu." Super simple × Crazy tasty.

SERVES 8-10

110g unsalted butter, softened
225g golden caster sugar
2 large eggs
4 ripe bananas, mashed
90ml buttermilk
1 tsp vanilla extract
285g plain flour
1 tsp bicarbonate of soda
½ tsp fine sea salt

You will need a 900g loaf tin

Preheat your oven to 180°C/Fan 160°C/Gas 4 and grease and line the loaf tin.

BANANA LOAF

Cream your butter and sugar together in a large bowl, using a hand-held or free-standing mixer, until light and fluffy.

Crack in your eggs, tip in your bananas and pour in your buttermilk and vanilla and give it a good mix.

Sift your flour, bicarbonate of soda and salt into a large bowl then fold it carefully into your cake mixture.

Spoon into the tin and bake for 45 minutes–1 hour, until golden brown and well risen.

Remove from the oven and leave to cool in the tin for 10–15 minutes, then turn out on to a wire rack to finish cooling.

Wait – you can't eat it yet! Leave it until it's cold.

> "YES, YOU HEARD ME, OR … SHOULD IT BE, YOU READ ME?"

LEVEL UP

Cut your loaf into slices no thicker than 2.5cm and toast 'em – under a grill or in a toaster – until they're golden and have a crispy surface, like bread basically.

Now you need to serve these pretty much straight away. Place some fried banana slices and a scoop of ice cream on each slice (see page 186 for my favourite recipe).

APRICOT ✳ BLUEBERRY ✳ PECAN SLABS

This is one of the first things I baked, successfully anyway,
so it had to go in the book.

MAKES ABOUT 12

3 tbsp maple syrup

150g vanilla yoghurt

350g apricots, skinned, halved
and stoned (or 1 × 410g tin
apricots, drained)

Crumble

50g unsalted butter, softened

6 heaped tbsp self-raising flour

3 tbsp demerara sugar

2½ tsp ground cinnamon

70g pecans, crushed

Traybake

200g unsalted butter, softened

115g golden caster sugar

110g light brown sugar

3 large eggs

45ml whole milk

225g self-raising flour

1 tsp baking powder

**You will need a 21 × 30cm
traybake tin**

Preheat oven to 180°C/Fan 160°C/
Gas 4 and line the traybake tin with
baking paper.

YOGHURT ✳ CRUMBLE

Mix your maple syrup and yoghurt
together in a small bowl.

Place all the ingredients for the crumble,
except the pecans, in a large bowl
and rub together until it becomes like
breadcrumbs.

Toss in the pecans and mix.

TRAYBAKE

Cream your butter and sugars together
in a large bowl, using a hand-held or free-
standing mixer, until light and fluffy.

Crack the eggs into a medium bowl and
add the milk. Whisk lightly then add to
the butter mixture and mix well.

Sift your flour and baking powder into
a separate bowl, turn the speed down
very low on your mixer, then add the
flour to the traybake mixture and mix
until creamy.

Spoon the mixture into the tin, level the
top and bake for 30 minutes.

TRAYBAKE TAKE TWO

Remove your traybake from the oven
and, moving quickly, spoon the maple
yoghurt over the top, then scatter
over your fruit and finish off with your
crumble.

Pop the traybake back in the oven for
another 20 minutes, until a skewer
inserted into the centre comes out clean.

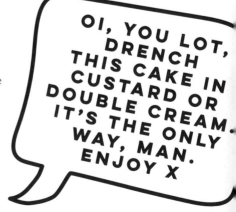

OI, YOU LOT,
DRENCH
THIS CAKE IN
CUSTARD OR
DOUBLE CREAM.
IT'S THE ONLY
WAY, MAN.
ENJOY X

WE ALL SCREAM FOR ...

I'm a massive fan of ice cream. On top of puddings, tarts,
pies – I mean, some people have it with custard as well! Crazy, right?
This ice cream recipe pretty much plays the same role as vanilla – it's a crowd
pleaser. But with its different combination of sugars, it gives the frozen
treat a deeper flavour. Ooo, get you, Liam, getting all cheffy.

SERVES 8

2 vanilla pods
360ml whole milk
465ml double cream
5 large egg yolks
75g soft light brown sugar
75g soft dark brown sugar

FLAVOUR YOUR MILK

Split your vanilla pods, scraping out the
seeds, and put both pods and seeds
into a large saucepan with the milk and
cream.

Place the pan over a medium heat
and bring to a gentle simmer. Leave to
simmer for 3–4 minutes.

MAKE YOUR CUSTARD

Meanwhile, place your egg yolks and
both sugars into a large bowl and mix
until well combined.

Turn the heat up under the milk and
bring it to the boil. Quickly pour your
milk into the egg yolks in a slow and
steady stream, whisking constantly.

Pour the custard back into the pan and
cook over a low heat, stirring all the time
with a large wooden spoon.

> "MATE, YOU DON'T
> WANT SCRAMBLED
> EGGS!"

Once it coats the back of the spoon it's
ready.

Pass the custard through a fine sieve and
discard the vanilla pods.

Leave the custard to cool completely.

Place a sheet of clingfilm on the surface
of the custard to prevent a skin from
forming, then pop in the fridge to chill
overnight.

> "YOU WANT YOUR
> CUSTARD TO BE AS
> COLD AS POSSIBLE
> FOR BEST RESULTS,
> TRUST ME."

ICE CREAM TIME

Get your ice cream maker going, then
slowly pour in the chilled custard.
Churn according to the manufacturer's
instructions, then pop it in a freezerproof container and place in the freezer
until solid. If you don't have an ice
cream maker, pour the mixture into a
freezerproof container, seal and place in
the freezer. After about an hour, stir well
to break up the ice crystals. Repeat
twice more.

VARIATIONS

Before you freeze the custard, you can
add squiggles of chocolate or caramel,
or fold ripples of lemon curd (see page
197) through it.

And, you can use this ice cream for
milkshakes ... Flick over.

SHAKING WITH THE MANDEM

If you didn't know already, I'm very easily pleased. But there's one rule you have to follow in order to be pals with me – you've got to love milkshakes. The possibilities are absolutely endless when it comes to ice cream and it's the same with milkshakes. I mean, the amount of toppers you can have on a milkshake is not even a joke. This recipe is just a guideline for making the perfect milkshake … And then you just have to express yourself – go nuts! This will make enough to fill four mason jars (pop them in the fridge to chill while you make the shake).

SERVES 4

720g We All Scream For … (see page 186) or use your favourite ice cream
320ml whole milk
300ml whipped cream

Put your ice cream and milk into a blender or jug (if you're using a stick blender) and blitz until smooth.

Pour into the jars and top with whipped cream. This'll be the foundation for your toppings …

"YOU CAN HAVE IT LIKE THAT BUT I SAY IT'S TIME FOR THE NEXT LEVEL UP …"

VARIATION 1: SUPER SALTED NUTTER

Add 120g salted caramel sauce (see page 198) and 100g peanut butter (see page 199) to the ice cream and milk before blending.

Use more caramel to swirl round the jars then top with whipped cream, pretzels and maybe a few chunks of brownie (see page 101). And more squiggles of caramel …

VARIATION 2: TANGY

Add 120–150g lemon curd (shop-bought or see page 197) to your ice cream and milk before blending.

Top with white chocolate shavings and crushed meringues.

VARIATION 3: YOU'RE TAKING THE MICK, LIAM

Add a generous slice of cheesecake (shop-bought or see page 47) to your ice cream and milk before blending.

Top with whipped cream and finish with another slice of cheesecake and a sprinkle of icing sugar.

SLUUUUUUUUURP . . . AND DON'T FEEL GUILTY.

WENSLEYDALE CRACKERS

Honestly, these crackers might just steal the show on your cheeseboard!

MAKES 20-25

100g wholemeal flour

50g self-raising flour

25g coarse oatmeal

100g unsalted butter, cold, cubed

100g Wensleydale cheese or mature Cheddar, grated

50g dried cranberries

1 large egg yolk

Preheat oven to 180°C/Fan 160°C/Gas 4.

Tip the flours and your oatmeal into a bowl and rub in the butter, just like with a crumble.

Pop in your cheese and dried cranberries and stir.

Add the egg yolk and start to bring everything together with a fork.

Tip the dough on to your work surface because you need to knead it until smooth . . . See what I did there?!

Place the dough between two sheets of baking paper and roll out to a thickness of about ¼cm, then cut the dough into any shape you want . . . Yes, any shape – express yourself.

Any leftovers? Just re-roll and cut out more shapes.

Bake for 15 minutes, until golden brown.

Remove from the oven and leave the crackers to firm before popping them on to a wire rack to cool.

CHEESEBOARD ESSENTIAL

Red onion chutney, pickle and a good cheese . . . Sorted!

MAKES 20-25

440g plain wholemeal flour, plus extra for dusting

2 tsp baking powder

125g coarse oatmeal

100g golden caster sugar

480g unsalted butter, cold, cubed

50ml cold water

You will need a 8cm cutter

Put all the ingredients, apart from the water, in a large bowl and rub in the butter until the mixture looks like breadcrumbs.

Add the water and mix until it forms a dough. Wrap in clingfilm and put in the fridge to rest for a couple of hours.

Preheat oven to 160°C/Fan 140°C/Gas 3 and line a baking tray with baking paper.

Take the dough out of the fridge, let it soften for 20 minutes, then roll it out on a lightly floured surface to a thickness of 5mm.

Using a 8cm cutter, cut out rounds and place them on the baking tray. Bake for 15 minutes, until golden brown.

Remove from the oven and leave the biscuits on the baking tray for about 6 minutes to firm up, then pop them on a wire rack to cool.

GOES WITH ANY CHEESE CRACKERS

Get dipping with hummus, spreading with butter or crumbling with cheese – take your pick!

MAKES 20-25

115g wholemeal flour

115g plain flour

115g semolina

1 tsp fine sea salt

½ tsp mixed herbs

55g sesame seeds

55g flaxseeds

55g pumpkin seeds, ground

215ml cold water

1 tbsp runny honey

3½ tbsp vegetable oil, plus extra for greasing

You will need a 10cm cutter

Combine all the dry ingredients in a large bowl.

Pour the water, honey and vegetable oil into a separate bowl and give them a quick whisk.

Add the dry ingredients to the wet ingredients and mix – you are looking for a firm dough. Bring it together and knead for a couple of minutes.

Leave to rest for 25 minutes.

Preheat oven to 180°C/Fan 160°C/Gas 4 and line 2 baking trays with baking paper.

Lightly grease your work surface with some vegetable oil and roll the dough to 2–3mm thickness.

Using a 10cm square cutter, cut out as many squares as you can. (If I were you, I wouldn't re-roll your scraps – the more they're worked the less of a snap they'll have. And you need that cheeky snap! So just put your scraps on an extra baking tray and those can be your edgy, cool, trendy crackers.)

Bake for 20 minutes, then treat your crackers like a cheesecake and turn off the oven and leave them inside with the door ajar for a minute. Close the door again and the crackers will continue to cook in the heat. You want that extra, extra crispiness, so leave them in the oven for another 10–15 minutes before taking them out and placing on a wire rack to cool.

NOW YOU WANT THESE CRACKERS TO BE SUPER THIN.

CRACKERS

WENSLEYDALE
CRACKERS

GOES WITH ANY
CHEESE CRACKERS

CHEESEBOARD
ESSENTIAL

FRUIT COMPOTE

I'm a massive fan of stewed fruits, especially on top of porridge
or yoghurt. This chunky, sweet but tart compote can go in the fridge and
be your cheeky stash towards your 5 a day …

MAKES ABOUT 1 LITRE

3 tbsp cornflour

4 tbsp water

500g frozen mixed berries

2 Bramley apples, peeled, cored and diced

1 Granny Smith apple, peeled, cored and diced

200g plums, stoned and halved

50g demerara sugar

50g unsalted butter

juice of 1 lemon

You will need 3 × 350ml airtight jars

Combine the cornflour and water in a small bowl to a paste.

Place all the ingredients, including the cornflour water, in a large pan over a medium heat.

Bring to a gentle simmer and cook for 20–25 minutes, until the fruit is soft but still holding its shape.

Transfer to the jars and, once cool, keep it in the fridge for up to 1 week.

BREAKFAST, LUNCH, DESSERT … YOU NAME IT.

FRUIT COMPOTE

ZINGY CURD

Use this in your cakes, biscuits, yoghurts, ice creams and cheesecakes.
If you're a lover of everything lemony, then here you go. You don't have to add the
orange zest but I think oranges and lemons are good pals, so figured
it was a good idea to give them a cameo.

MAKES ABOUT 800ML

zest of 2 large lemons
zest of 2 large oranges
juice of 6 large lemons
200g unsalted butter, cubed
3 tbsp runny honey
400g caster sugar
6 large eggs, beaten

You will need 2 × 400ml airtight jars

Zest two of the lemons and place in a large saucepan with the orange zest and the juice from all six lemons.

Add the butter, honey and sugar and place over a low heat, until the butter has melted. Don't forget to stir, you want to make sure the sugar has dissolved, too.

Remove from the heat and leave to cool for a couple of minutes – you don't want to add the eggs while the mixture is too hot.

Whisk in the eggs and return the pan to the heat. Cook over a low heat for 5 minutes, whisking constantly, until thick, gloopy and glossy.

Remove from the heat and pass the curd through a sieve into a measuring jug.

Transfer to the jars and, once cool, keep it in the fridge for up to 1 week.

BAM!

ZINGY CURD

THE SALTED CARAMEL

The sauce of all sauces – it goes on everything, even your sausages, enough said.

MAKES ABOUT 600ML

65ml water
230g caster sugar
85g unsalted butter
130ml double cream
½ tsp vanilla extract
fine sea salt, to taste

You will need 2 × 300ml airtight jars

Place the water in a saucepan, then slowly add the caster sugar a little bit at a time, whisking until it's all in.

I do this because sometimes the sugar isn't evenly distributed in the pan when it starts boiling and it goes really weird and annoying. To use another word … crystallisation.

Place the pan over a medium heat and leave it alone until the sugar has turned a deep amber colour.

"NOW THIS PART CAN MAKE OR BREAK YOUR CARAMEL. DON'T BE SCARED TO GO A DEEP, DARK AMBER BROWN. YOU WANT IT SWEET BUT WITH A SLIGHTLY BITTER SWAG TO IT."

Remove from the heat and add the butter.

Return to the heat and stir until the butter is completely melted and well mixed in.

Remove from the heat again and add the cream and vanilla and mix again. Return to the heat for another 10 seconds and then remove.

TASTE TEST

Some recipes tell you how much salt to add to your salted caramel but, NAH, not mine. It's all down to preference – start by adding ¼ teaspoon, then a little more each time. When you've reached your perfect amount … I'll appear on your shoulder and say, "That's the one, bud!" Only joking.

Once it's passed the taste test, transfer to the jars and keep it in the fridge for up to 1 week.

ENJOY!

HONEY NUT ROASTED

I absolutely love peanuts and one of my favourite kinds is honey-roasted. I've never come across it in a peanut butter … Well, until now, that is. You can slap this on your toast, spread it on your bananas, add it to your curries, the lot.

MAKES ABOUT 600ML

500g honey-roasted peanuts
4 tbsp runny honey
1 tsp fine sea salt
1–2 tbsp peanut oil

You will need 2 × 300ml airtight jars

Preheat oven to 200°C/Fan 180°C/Gas 6.

Tip the peanuts on to a baking tray and roast for 10 minutes.

Remove from the oven and leave to cool.

Toss your peanuts into a food-processor and blitz for about 10 minutes, until a smooth paste. Scrape down the sides of your bowl from time to time.

Add the honey and salt then drizzle in the peanut oil until you get the right consistency.

Transfer to the jars and keep it in the fridge for up to 1 week.

CLASSIC SMOOTH: BLITZ 450G SHELLED PEANUTS IN A FOOD-PROCESSOR UNTIL SMOOTH. ADD 4 TEASPOONS OF RUNNY HONEY AND 1 TEASPOON OF FINE SEA SALT. GRADUALLY DRIZZLE IN AROUND 1-2 TABLESPOONS OF PEANUT OIL UNTIL YOU GET THE RIGHT CONSISTENCY.

HONEY NUT ROASTED

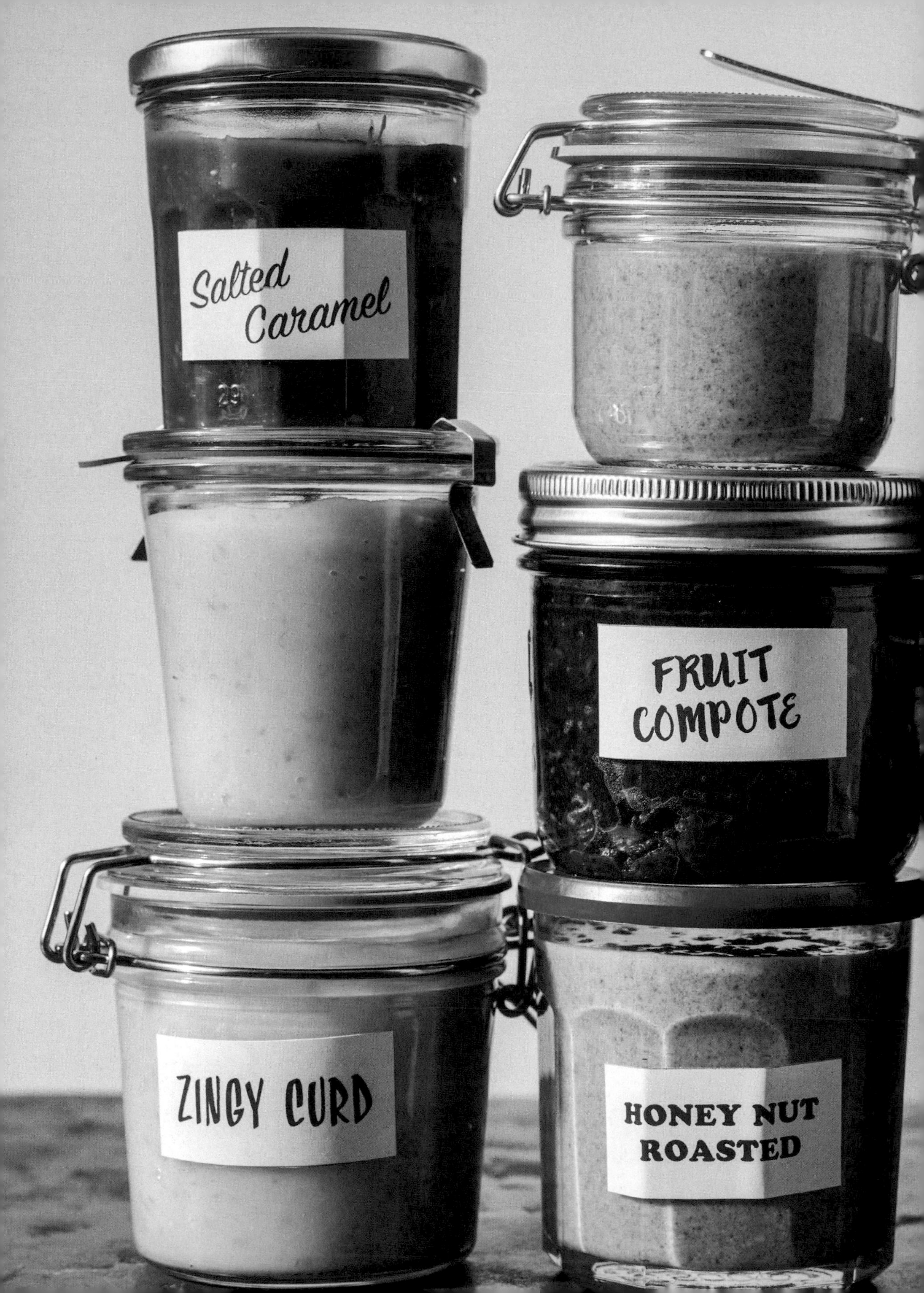
Salted Caramel
FRUIT COMPOTE
ZINGY CURD
HONEY NUT ROASTED

CHEEKY
TREATS
ASSEMBLE!

TEKKERS

All right, so to become an absolute master of this book, there
are a few things you need to know how to do. Imagine this book is
a massive game, these are the cheat codes!

BAIN-MARIE

This is just a saucepan with a few centimetres of boiling
water in it with another bowl over the top. You can use
your free-standing mixer bowl for this but make sure the
water is not touching the bottom. Keep the pan over a
low heat while you melt/whisk.

MELTING CHOCOLATE

Melt the chocolate over a bain-marie or in a microwave. If
you do the latter then make sure you heat the chocolate
in 20-second bursts, stirring after each interval, so that you
don't burn it.

DEEP-FRYING

When deep-frying it's best to wear long sleeves to
protect yourself from splashes and make sure kids are out
of the way.

Fill a deep-fat fryer or large saucepan to the max point
with your oil and heat it to the desired temperature – use
a food thermometer in a large saucepan. Get a tray lined
with kitchen paper ready to absorb the excess oil.

Carefully place whatever you're frying inside – do this in
batches so the temperature doesn't drop too much. Use
tongs to flip it and use them again to pick out the fried
treat. Place it on the prepared tray. Repeat this process
until everything is fried.

SHORTCRUST PASTRY

Tip the flour, salt and butter into a food-processor and
pulse until it resembles fine breadcrumbs. You can do
this by hand – use your fingertips to rub the butter into
the flour.

Pour the egg and cold water into a small bowl and
beat lightly. Add to the butter and flour, with the motor
running, until it starts to come together into a ball. Tip the
pastry onto the work surface and gently bring it together.

CLASSIC SIMPLE
SPONGE TECHNIQUE

Add the butter and sugars to a large bowl and beat using
a hand-held or free-standing mixer with your beater
attachment until light and fluffy. Crack in your eggs one at
a time. If the mixture begins to curdle, just pop in a couple
tablespoons of the flour to bring it back together. Once
all the eggs are incorporated, turn the speed down very
low and add your dry ingredients. Finally, loosen your cake
mixture with milk or vanilla extract.

CLASSIC CHOCOLATE
SPONGE TECHNIQUE

Sift your caster sugar, plain flour, cocoa powder, salt
and bicarbonate of soda into a large bowl. Add in your
chocolate chips, if using.

In a separate bowl, combine your wet ingredients –
coffee, buttermilk, vegetable oil, eggs – and give them a
light whisk.

Now add the dry ingredients to the wet ingredients in
3 batches, mixing thoroughly after each addition.

WEIGHING CAKE MIXTURE

You should want to be exact and have the sponges equal,
so tip the mixture into a separate bowl to weigh it and
then divide by the number of tins.

CAKE BUILDING

Once the cakes have cooled, using a cake leveller or a sharp knife, trim the top off all the cakes so they are level. Using a board slightly bigger than your sponges, spread a small amount of buttercream on to the board and place your first layer of sponge on to it. Place that board on top of a turntable, if you have one.

CHEQUERING

Use a cutter to cut a large circle out of the middle of each of the cakes. Make sure you press down firmly so you achieve a clean cut. Remove the circles and set aside. Get a smaller circle cutter and cut out smaller circles into the circles you have already cut. Place the rings of one cake in another, alternating the colours.

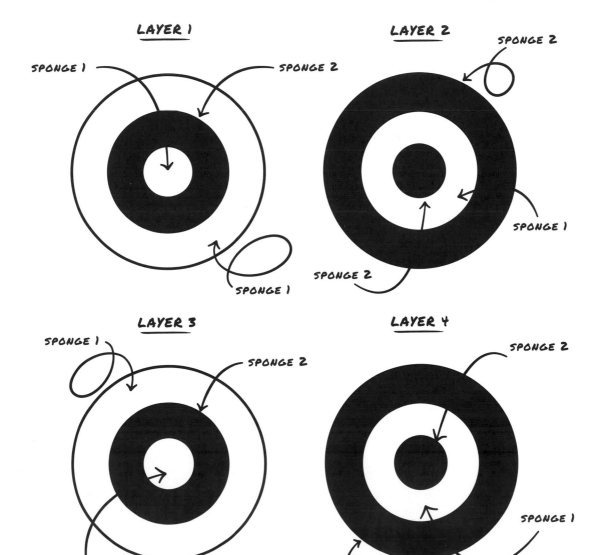

CLASSIC BUTTERCREAM TECHNIQUE

Beat your butter in a large bowl with your hand-held or free-standing mixer until it is light and pale. Sift your icing sugar into a separate bowl, then add it to the butter in 3 stages, beating after each addition. Beat for a couple more minutes, scraping down the sides of the bowl from time to time. Add milk or other flavouring to loosen the buttercream.

SWISS MERINGUE BUTTERCREAM

Prepare a bain-marie – add your egg whites to the bowl then pour in your caster sugar. Get your whisk and begin to stir everything together until the sugar has fully dissolved. The best way to check this is the fingertip test. Just rub a bit of the mixture in between your fingers, if you can't feel any sugar, it's ready.

Remove the bowl from the heat and using a hand-held whisk or your whisk attachment in your free-standing mixer, whisk on a medium–high speed for about 10 minutes, or until it's cool. You should be aiming for super fluffy clouds of meringue.

Add butter chunks to your Swiss meringue and whisk on a medium speed – take your time with this stage. Show your buttercream some love – the more patient you are adding the butter, the nicer your buttercream will be.

GANACHE

Pour your cream into a saucepan and place over a gentle heat. Measure your chocolate into a large bowl and, once the cream is just simmering, pour it over the chocolate and leave it to melt for a couple of minutes. Begin to stir with a wooden spoon, stirring from the centre outwards. Continue to stir until it's a glossy, smooth consistency.

PERFECTLY WHIPPED CREAM

I always stuff this up – I over-whip the cream. So my advice – buy more double cream than you actually need just in case! The trick is, it's more instinct than anything, you want to stop a couple of seconds before you think it's actually ready; have a look at the consistency, if it's a little under-whipped continue in 5-second bursts until it's ready to go.

CRUMB COAT

A crumb coat ensures your final layer of buttercream doesn't have any crumbs coming through. Using a palette knife, cake scraper and a turntable, coat the sides and top of the cake with a thin layer of buttercream until it's covered. If you don't have a turntable, you can place your cake on a sturdy large board. After you've done the crumb coat, place your cake in the fridge for at least an hour to set.

PREPARING A PIPING BAG

If you're using a disposable bag, fill the bag with the tip down – you can pop it in a mug or glass to make it easier to fill, just with the top of the bag over the edge. When ready to pipe, cut off the tip to make a hole to your preferred size.

If you are using a nozzle, snip the tip off a new bag and push the nozzle all the way down to the end of the bag so that it fits snugly, then fill with your buttercream.

GETTING PERFECT CIRCLES WHEN YOU PIPE

Use a pastry cutter and draw around it on to baking paper with a pencil to make the circles. When you place the paper back on the baking tray, flip it over so it acts like a guide when you are piping.

FLURRY ICING EFFECT

Snip the edges of the piping bags and, with the cake on a turntable, pipe streaks of buttercream alternating the different colours, until the whole of cake is covered. Then, using a palette knife, smooth the sides and top and the icing gets a flurry effect.

INDEX

COOKERY NOTES

☆ Standard level spoon measurements are used in all recipes.

    1 tablespoon = one 15ml spoon
    1 teaspoon = one 5ml spoon

☆ Some recipes contain raw or partially cooked eggs. Pregnant women, the elderly, babies and toddlers, and people who are unwell should avoid these recipes.

☆ If a recipe calls for a small or hard-to-weigh amount of salt, remember that ½ teaspoon fine salt weighs 2.5g and ¼ teaspoon weighs 1.25g. If you are using sea salt it is best to crush the flakes into a fine powder before measuring and adding to the recipe (unless otherwise specified).

☆ Ovens should be preheated to the specific temperature. Don't forget that ovens vary – from the front to the back of the oven, as well as between top and bottom shelves – so an oven thermometer is very useful. Get to know your oven and where the 'hot spots' are. Make sure your oven gloves are dry when you are using them.

☆ Be very careful when deep-frying – keep children out of the kitchen and protect yourself by wearing long sleeves, eye protection and keeping your face away from the pan.

CONVERSION CHARTS

All equivalents are rounded, for practical convenience.

WEIGHT

25g	1oz
50g	2oz
100g	3½oz
150g	5oz
200g	7oz
250g	9oz
300g	10oz
400g	14oz
500g	1lb 2oz
1kg	2¼lb

VOLUME (LIQUIDS)

5ml		1 tsp
15ml		1 tbsp
30ml	1fl oz	⅛ cup
60ml	2fl oz	¼ cup
75ml		⅓ cup
120ml	4fl oz	½ cup
150ml	5fl oz	⅔ cup
175ml		¾ cup
250ml	8fl oz	1 cup
1 litre	1 quart	4 cups

VOLUME (DRY SERVES – AN APPROXIMATE GUIDE)

butter	1 cup (2 sticks) = 225g
rolled oats	1 cup = 100g
fine powders (e.g. flour)	1 cup = 125g
nuts (e.g. hazelnuts)	1 cup = 125g
seeds (e.g. sesame)	1 cup = 160g
dried fruit (e.g. raisins)	1 cup = 150g
large dried legumes (e.g. chickpeas)	1 cup = 170g
grains, granular goods and small dried legumes (e.g. rice, quinoa, sugar, lentils)	1 cup = 200g
grated cheese	1 cup = 100g

LENGTH

1cm	½ inch
2.5cm	1 inch
20cm	8 inches
25cm	10 inches
30cm	12 inches

OVEN TEMPERATURES

Celsius	Fahrenheit
140	275
150	300
160	325
180	350
190	375
200	400
220	425
230	450

THANK YOU

Okay, okay, I promise not to cry …

Well, that's the end of *Cheeky Treats* Vol. 1. Vol. 2? Who knows! ;-P

I'm not really good at this part because it's pretty much
saying goodbye … for now.

If I said thank you to everyone, that would be another book in itself.

But thank you to all my family, friends and everyone
who has supported me through this journey because, let's be fair,
without you lot I wouldn't be doing this now.

Remember … this is only the beginning.

BIG LOVE,

 X

First published in Great Britain in 2018 by Hodder & Stoughton

An Hachette UK company

2

Copyright © Liam Charles 2018
Photography by Haarala Hamilton © Hodder & Stoughton 2018

A CIP catalogue record for this title is available from the British Library

Hardback ISBN 978 1 473 68720 2
eBook ISBN 978 1 473 68721 9

Colour origination by Born Group
Printed and bound in Germany by Mohn Media

Hodder & Stoughton policy is to use papers that are natural, renewable
and recyclable products and made from wood grown in sustainable forests.
The logging and manufacturing processes are expected to conform to the
environmental regulations of the country of origin.

The publisher would like to thank Bear & Bear for supplying the cake stand
featured in Ooo Fancy on page 136.

Hodder & Stoughton Ltd
Carmelite House
50 Victoria Embankment
London EC4Y 0DZ

www.hodder.co.uk

Editorial director: Nicky Ross
Project editor: Natalie Bradley
Copy-editor: Jo Roberts-Miller
Art direction and design concept: Superfantastic
Designer: Nicky Barneby
Photographers: Liz and Max Haarala Hamilton
Food stylists: Samantha Dixon and Katy Ross
Props stylist: Anna Wilkins
Production manager: Claudette Morris